I0211751

LETTERS OF A LOVESICK BRIDE

Prayers and Poems from a Bride Captivated
& Longing for King Jesus

+10 Letters from the author specifically for you!

JANELLE ANDONIE

Copyright © 2021 by Janelle Andonie
Author Photo Credit: Carolina Caicedo

Published by Clay Bridges in Houston, TX
www.ClayBridgesPress.com

All rights reserved. No part of this publication may be reproduced, stored in a retrieval system, or transmitted in any form by any means, electronic, mechanical, photocopy, recording, or otherwise, with the prior permission of the publisher, except as provided for by USA copyright law.

ISBN: 978-1-953300-42-3
eISBN:978-1-953300-43-0

Sales: Most Clay Bridges titles are available in special quantity discounts. Custom imprinting or excerpting can also be done to fit special needs. Contact Clay Bridges at Info@ClayBridgesPress.com.

For my mother,
who taught me how to love Jesus well.

CONTENTS

Prayers/Poems

Letters From The Author To You

1

I Want to Be Lovesick For You

Jesus,

I don't want to fall out of love with you
I don't want to grow numb to your presence
If I ever do, take me back to when it was only you and me,
And remind me of all the reasons why I fell in love with you

I want to forever wake up expecting your nearness
Go about my day longing to be more attuned to your voice
And as I finish my day, I want to be known for running to your feet,
And patiently waiting for you to satisfy me

Like a lovesick bride
I wait for you to meet me
I long for you to speak to me
And I wait for just one touch of your presence, for it can change everything

For you created me to be in love with you
You wired my DNA to be attracted to you
And you know how to pull on my heart strings
So meet me & cure my lovesickness

How sweet are these moments with you
I always want to ache for you
I always want to be lovesick for you
So don't let me fall out of love with you

Scripture: Matthew 22:37-38; Psalm 63 (TPT)

Application: Read Psalm 63, especially in the Passion Translation, and meditate on David's zeal for God. Do you share that same zeal? Does your life reflect that passion for your God? Even Jesus reminds us in Matthew 22 of the first and greatest commandment which is to love God with all our heart, soul, and mind. Friend, He longs to be in a relationship with you. He delights when you go to Him in worship and praise. And He wants you to be lovesick for Him - soul, mind, and heart. And if you are not there yet, there is no condemnation for He wired you to long for Him. He only asks for your yes and an open heart. So today, meditate on His goodness and let your faith rise. Then, commit to spending time with Him and ask Him to make you lovesick for Him. It's worth it.

2

Captivated

Jesus,

With just one look, I am already captivated by you. A look at your fiery yet merciful eyes. It's all it takes for me to be bewitched by you. A look at your snowy white hair like wool. It's all it takes for me to be allured to you.

Just like the four living creatures gaze upon you day and night, let me never stop fixing my eyes on you. Just like they have never stopped calling you "holy holy," let me forever join with them in worship. Just as they keep getting new revelations of who you are, let me see you in a different way every time. Just as the 24 elders lay down their crowns before you, let me lay down all lesser lovers down at your feet.

And when I look at your face, I am at peace. I become content. I am in awe. I become mesmerized. I am undone. And I am *captivated*. I realize nothing else matters because you are the One thing my heart desires. You are the One thing I seek. You are the One thing everyone is looking for. It's you my King. And it will always be you.

Give me the desire to wake up and look at you. To go about my day and think about you instead of letting your words collect dust on the shelf. To lay down and cherish the moments spent with you that day. I want to be captivated by you. It's you. It's always been you. The Holy One. The captivating One.

Scripture: Rev 1:12-18; Rev 4:8-11

Application: Read the scriptures in Revelations 4 and let this scene give you a picture of the holiness of Jesus. Let this ignite your spirit to want to join in the living creatures in finding new revelations of His nature and join the elders in laying down their crowns before His feet. Friend, when we focus our eyes on Jesus, nothing else matters. The cares of this world start subsiding and His peace increases. So ask yourself today, "Am I fixing my eyes on Jesus or on things of this world? What crown do I have to lay down today to be able to let Jesus captivate me? To make God the center of my life?"

3

Give Me Your Desires

Jesus,

Thank you for giving me the free will to make decisions and go after what I desire, but I want your desires and longings more than mine. Give me a revelation of what you desire for me, for others, and for this world. Help me burn for what burns you.

I give you permission to interrupt the trivial activities of my day and place your desires in me. I give you permission to breathe what you yearn for through dreams and visions. I give you permission to break down any walls preventing me from seeing what pulls on your heart strings.

I give you permission to water the soil of my heart to make it fertile for what you have placed in me. Take any desire that I have that is not rooted and grounded in you, and give me your desires for me. For I know that what you desire is better than anything my earthly heart could long for.

Thank you for trusting me enough to share those treasures with me. I receive, steward, and will intercede for them humbly, my King.

Scripture: Psalm 37:4; Ecclesiastes 3:11 (AMP); Jeremiah 29:11

Application: In Ecclesiastes 3:11 (AMP) God tells us how God has "planted eternity [a sense of divine purpose] in the human heart [a mysterious longing which nothing under the sun can satisfy, except God]..." You see, God has already placed desires in your heart, but without an intimate relationship with Him, we can't be satisfied nor discern His desires from our desires. He is the one who leads us, directs our path, and keeps watering the soil of our heart so we can fulfill those desires. But sometimes our desires are based on what we see in this world. I encourage you, ask God to reveal in your heart what desires He has placed and what desires do not line up with His will for your life. And remember, no matter how scary it is to let go of certain dreams, you can trust He has something better and that He knows best. He is your good Father.

4

My Soul, Don't You Know?

Jesus,

Let me trust you in the silence
Let me trust you in the storm
Let me still believe,
You have my world under control

So I align my soul with my Spirit
I decide to not live by my flesh
I do not look to my circumstances
And I speak to my soul rest

Soul,
Don't you think He knows what you need?
Don't you think He knows your desires?
Don't you think He made you intricately with likes & dislikes?
Don't you think He knows your every thought and emotion?
Don't you think He has planned your story since the beginning?
Don't you think He knows your every move by heart?
Don't you think He fights for you while you are still?
Don't you think He cares about every detail of your story?
Don't you think He rejoices in knowing you? Delights in spending time with you?

Don't you think He knows what you want but does not want you to settle?
Don't you think He is constantly wanting to be close? Wanting to spoil you? Wanting to love you well? To shower you with blessings?

And just like that my soul quiets
And I am reminded,
This is what it's like to be fully known, loved, and cared for
You can rest, my soul

Scripture: Psalm 131 (AMP), Psalm 139

Application: Have you ever been in a situation where you can't see God in anything? You feel forgotten. Your emotions take over and you start living from your soul, not your Spirit. Friend, I've been there. Today I want to remind you that God has never left you nor forsaken you! He has his eyes on you. So when trouble, disappointments, or setbacks come, we have to decide to live by God's truth. Take the psalmist in Psalm 131, He spoke to His soul and declared what He knew was truth in the face of trial. So I invite you to make a list of truths that are hard for you to believe and speak them to your soul so it can be weaned. Let's encourage ourselves in the Lord.

5

Your Presence: Holy Spirit

Jesus,

Thank you for your Holy Spirit. Thank you for allowing and blessing us, mere humans, to be the home of your Spirit of truth. Thank you for marking us with your holy seal. We do not take it lightly.

We love your presence invading and encompassing all of our hearts. Every empty space. Every crack. Every unsatisfied chamber. We delight in it more than getting to see a cloud by day or fire by night. More than only being able to go into the Holiest of Holiest once a year. Having you this close is the best gift.

Thank you Holy Spirit for being the constant one. No matter what we are going through, you are there. If we are in despair, you are there with fresh hope. If we are overjoyed, you are there rejoicing with us. If we are under sin, you are there lovingly convicting us. If we need direction, you are there showing us the way. If we need a breakthrough, you are there interceding for us through wordless groans. We bless you today.

We pray that we would be good stewards of your temple God. Help us not grieve you. We want to host you well.

Scripture: John 14:16-17; Exodus 13:20-22; Hebrews 9:7; Romans 8:26; Ephesians 1:13; Ephesians 4:30

Application: When Jesus died on the cross and rose back to life, He gave us access to the Holy Spirit. Before then, the Israelites could only access God's presence in the temple through a high priest. The good news is that now when we accept Jesus as Lord and Savior, He seals us with the mark of His Holy Spirit. He is now living in us and we have become His temple. So today ask yourself, what can I do to make my body a Holy Temple for the Holy Spirit? How can I avoid grieving Him in my daily walk?

6

In the Hiding

God,

Thank you for the hiding season.

In the hiding, where no one is around
In the dark, when no one can see me
In the wilderness, where I don't see a way
I will worship you, until the end of days

In the drought, while looking for living water
In the fiery furnace, while you refine me
In the process, when it's only you and I
I will grow closer and draw nearer to you

When I am not favored
When I am not recognized
When I don't have a title,
I will rejoice, for you are with me

What else could I desire?
What is better than a Father who is so jealous for my heart?
What is better than a God who longs for my affections?
What is better than a lover who isolates me in the wilderness to
have my undivided attention?

What else could I desire than you and I?
What else than your tangible presence?
So I remind my soul, nothing is better
For you are more than enough

Scripture: Hosea 2; 1 Peter 1:6-9; Psalm 16:2

Application: How many of us have been in a hiding season? We feel unseen, unappreciated, and like we don't measure up. But I have learned that it is in this season where we are refined by God, learn to depend solely on Him, and learn how to steward His presence well. It's where intimacy is birthed. Just like God had to take Israel to the wilderness to be able to get their eyes back on Him, so does He mercifully hides and isolates us from lesser lovers to get us to fix our eyes on Him once again. So go back to your last hiding season and remember how He met you there. What did God teach you in it?

7

Fairytale Story

God,

You are the fairytale story. You sent your only Son to die for me. To pay a price with His precious blood. To rescue me from sin, darkness, and everything that wants to exalt itself above your name so that I could be set apart for your name.

While everyone else is looking to the things of this world to rescue and satisfy them, I rejoice because I know the true love story. I dance before you because I know the true fairytale ending. I shout praises to your name because I know how the book ends.

It's with your Son Jesus. He is God yet human. He is lowly as a lamb yet powerful as God Almighty. He is a gentleman who comes in only when asked, but full of authority. Mercy oozes from His eyes yet justness shows in His character.

Who is this man Jesus who can give living water so that I do not thirst again? Who is this man Jesus who loves me enough to lay down His life for me? Who is this man Jesus who is still committed to me after 2,021 years? Who is this man Jesus who is loving enough to love me as I am yet patient enough to wait for me to become more like Him?

And when we, His bride, are ready, He is coming as the bridegroom on a white horse. His name is Faithful and True and every knee has to bow before Him. He wears many crowns and in His thigh He has written "KING OF KINGS AND LORD OF LORDS." And His bride awaits Him clothed in fine linen, white and pure.

He will come. Do not doubt it. The wedding awaits an appointed time. He will marry His bride. He will rescue us. Eden will be restored. And it will be finished. Thank you for this eternal Happily Ever After, King Jesus.

Scripture: Revelation 19:6-21

Application: How many of us have waited for a man to come sweep us off our feet to have a happily ever after and be fulfilled? How many of us have based our happiness on a Disney fairytale story? Friend, let's start shifting our gaze and realize that God was the creator of the most epic love story: Jesus, the Son of God, laying down His life to be in relationship with you and me. That my friend is a love worth waiting for and worth rejoicing over. So today, reflect on how we, the bride, can be ready for King Jesus's return and make a commitment to always find our hope in His coming instead of in earthly person or thing.

8

I Need You

Jesus,

When pride comes in and I feel like I can do it on my own. When I think I have the strength necessary to accomplish my goals. You lovingly enter in. You humble me. You remind me of how much I need you. You remind me that it is by your Holy Spirit and not by my strength.

Just like you humbled the Israelites for 40 years in the wilderness, you humble me. Just how you humbled Moses by not allowing him to enter the Promised land, you humble me. Just like you humbled Adam and Eve in the garden, you humble me. You graciously show me how there is room to bow down low at your feet. And I'm thankful for it.

You lovingly show me I am not as different from them as I think I am. But in the midst of all, you don't condemn me. Instead, you remind me how you willingly gave yourself so I can freely receive grace. Not in my own effort, but by your sacrifice.

Thank you for allowing me to need you. To depend on you. To be humble towards you.

I need you.

Scripture: Zechariah 4:6; John 3:16; James 4:10

Application: Sometimes we can feel like we have the strength and wisdom to accomplish our goals on our own. We rely on past successes and build our confidence. But let me remind you how in James 4:6 we learn how God shows favor to the humble and opposes the proud. In the greek, the word humble means to "confess and deplore one's spiritual littleness and unworthiness."[1] You see, without God we are nothing. It does not matter how good we are at something, it all goes back to God, who has blessed us with those talents and has allowed us to succeed in them. Friend, I invite you to acknowledge that before God today, take a posture of reverence and humble yourself before God. Let Him know how you are well aware that you need Him in your life. This could be bowling down, saying a prayer, repenting for your sins, or however, the Lord leads.

---

[1]   https://biblehub.com/greek/5013.htm

9

There's Hope

Jesus,

I sit with a weary soul and troubled mind
Doubting if what you said would happen
Letting my circumstances speak louder than your voice
Seeing how my present does not line up with your promises

But then I hear you calling me by name
You draw me close — closer than the air I breathe
You remove the blindfold from my eyes
And you speak louder than the lies

And when I feel the wind of your presence
You remind me that there is hope
And when you show me visions of what's to come
You remind me that you are always working behind the scenes

And then I can hope again
For you are the God *of* hope
Who fills me with joy and peace
As I believe in you and your faithfulness

For you are faithful to fill my cup to overflow
You are faithful to renew my strength

So I do not grow weary nor get discouraged
For you are the hope of glory

And once you've breathed hope in me
My soul becomes anchored in you
And faith rises up, the kind that is unwavering
The unshakeable one that only comes from you alone

Scripture: Romans 15:13; Isaiah 40:31; Hebrews 6:13-20

Application: I wrote this in a season when my hope tank was depleted. And even though that might seem like a negative situation to be in, I've learned that when we hit rock bottom the only way we can go is up. So I encourage you, when you feel like there is no hope, go to God. He is faithful to fill us back up. For He *is* hope! So friend, ask Him to fill your tank of hope today! He is faithful and pleased to do it and fill your cup to overflow.

10

Rest

God,

Thank you for your gift of rest. Thank you for making it available to us every minute, every hour, and every day — even in the midst of our day's busyness. Lord, remind us that because you live in us, we have full access to your peace.

Thank you that for You, rest is an act of faith. It's a place where we don't have to strive. A place where we don't have to ponder on the what if's or should have's. Instead, it's a place where we can remain confident and trust in your sovereignty.

Just like you provided heavenly bread for the Israelites every morning, so will you provide what I need every day. Without me striving. Without me having to work for it. You give it freely. You give it generously.

Lord, I pray that you would help me understand that it's okay to rest even when I do not have all the answers. Let the truth of your provision sink in my heart — that when I need instructions and answers you will provide fresh manna from Heaven. And because of this, I can rest in your peace. And I can rest knowing that you are a faithful Father.

Scripture: Isaiah 26:3, Exodus 16; Matthew 11:28

Application: Sometimes we believe the lie that we can't rest until we know all the answers or we have it all together. But I want to remind you, God delights in our rest. For Him, it is an act of faith. He delights when we submit all of our anxieties and worries unto Him and let Him take the load. He loves it when we are still and know that He is God. Just as He asked the Israelites to rest on the 7th day, so does He want us to rest in Him. And remember, even though they rested, He still met their needs by sending them double manna. You see, He delights in us trusting Him with our needs. So ask yourself, are you living from a place of rest or striving? What decisions can you make today to help you live from a place of rest during the week?

11

You See Me Righty

God,

Thank you for bringing the best in me. Thank you for your encouragement — that not only builds me up, but it pierces my heart. It renews my mind. It leaves a mark. And I am forever changed.

Thank you for your sweet words that come crashing in my heart like mighty waves — full of love and truth. They not only break down walls I have placed, but they invade every space that has been filled with a lie.

And when I feel afraid, you see me brave. When I feel unqualified, you call me equipped. When I feel weak, you call me strong. Thank you for reminding me of who I am in you. Thank you for seeing me rightly.

I pray for a deeper revelation of how you see me King. I give you permission to open my eyes to the spiritual realm. Introduce me to the person you have created me to be. Help me become who you say I am. And I pray that it'd be all through the Holy Spirit's strength and not in my might.

Scripture: 1 Corinthians 1:27-29; 2 Corinthians 5:17; Zechariah 4:6

Application: Isn't it fascinating how God uses the foolish things of the world to shame the wise? He chooses to use each one of us, regardless of our sins and iniquities, to serve and love Him. Why? Because through Jesus' sacrifice we have been made righteous. God does not see our sinful nature but rather, He sees us rightly. Take time today to ponder on how Jesus' perfect sacrifice made this possible. Praise God choosing you even when you are not holy and perfect as He is. And finally, ask God to reveal how He sees you and who He has called you to be, no matter what the present circumstances say. Now, write it below in faith.

Circumstances	Who God Says I am
_____	_____
_____	_____
_____	_____

12

God's Love

God,

Thank you Lord for your unconditional love. A love that is patient and kind. A love that does not envy or boast. A love that keeps no record of wrongs. A love that does not treat us as our sins deserve but rather has blotted them out and has separated them from us as far as the east is from the west.

How is it possible that love so irrational and reckless exists? A love that breaks through the walls of hardened hearts, seeps in, and covers every empty space. A love that binds up fear, commands it to leave and invites in courage. A love that does not ask for much in return, but rather delights in simple communion. I love that willingly encamps around those you have chosen. A love that is no respecter of a person.

My God, what kind of love is this? That you would give your only Son to die for us while we were still sinners so that we can be close? What kind of love is this? That you keep your covenant of love to a thousand generations of those who love you. What kind of love is this? That we can not run away from but rather, chases us down.

We are forever grateful for this gift, Lord. Thank you for letting us receive and steward your love to be able to pour it out on others. We love because you first loved us.

Scripture: 1 Corinthians 13:4-5, Psalm 103:9-12; 1 John 4:18-19; Deuteronomy 7:9

Application: Reminisce on God's love for you today. Remind yourself of all the times He has loved you well, especially when you did not deserve it. Thank Him for His love. Boast in it. Rejoice in it. And most importantly, share it. Remember, we can now love others because He loved us first. Write down the names of 3 people who you repeatedly engage with who do not know of this love and pray for their hearts to be softened towards God.

1. _____

2. _____

3. _____

13

You Are Trustworthy

God,

What kind of God are you? One that is faithful even in my faithlessness. Because of this, I choose to praise you in the valley as much as I do in the mountaintop. I choose today to trust you in the process — even when all the pieces do not add up.

I choose to trust your ability to give me a clean perspective. I choose to believe that you are the same God today, yesterday, and forever. I choose to lay my feelings aside and let faith ignite my heart. I choose to let it seep into my thoughts and quiet my soul.

Because you are worthy of my trust. Because even when things don't make sense, you are faithful to make all things work out for my good. Because even when I don't see a way, you are faithful to make a way. Because even when it seems impossible, you are able to make the impossible a possibility in my life. It's who you are. The Trustworthy One.

Scripture: 2 Timothy 2:13, Hebrews 13:8, Psalm 131:2, Romans 8:28, Matthew 19:26

Applications: In what areas of your life are you having a hard time trusting God in? Today, I want to invite you to ask God to help you release your control over them and trust Him with them. I encourage you, find 3 verses about releasing control and trusting God. Then, ponder on them this week. Let God's word sink deep in your heart and let Him speak truth and quiet your soul.

14

Thank You for Relationship

God,

Thank you for listening. For conversation. For responses. Thank you for being attentive to my cry for help. For looking around the earth for those who need strengthening and stopping for me. Looking at me. Investing in me. Thank you for cherishing those prayers. For guarding them in a golden bowl — for they are a fragrant aroma to you.

So I thank you for the answered prayers, but mostly for the unanswered ones. Thank you for knowing and only giving me what is best for me, and aligning my heart with your timeline. Thank you for not giving in to my whims and tantrums. Thank you for knowing better and being strong for me when I could not understand your decision. Thank you for gently saying no. I cherish those unanswered prayers as much as the yes? Your corrections are as sweet as your affections.

Thank you for those times when I didn't know what to pray for. Thank you for those times when I didn't have the words or the strength. You met me there and continue to meet me. You fill up the space between my emptiness and your deitiness. You fill up the gap between my faithlessness and your faithfulness. You come. You pray for me. And you intercede for me. Thank you for this relationship.

> **Scripture:** Psalm 34:15, Revelations 5:8, 2 Chronicles 16:9

> **Applications:** Take time to meditate on the fact that we can have a relationship with the Most High God. Not everyone in this world has that anchor to hold on to. Now, think about all those times He was faithful by answering your prayers. He did not have to, but He chose to. But also meditate on those prayers that He did not answer. How can you see His goodness, protection, and mercy in those?

	Unanswered Prayers	**His Goodness in the Midst**
1.	_____	_____
2.	_____	_____
3.	_____	_____

15

There's Grace

Jesus,

You took my sins upon yourself. You allowed yourself to be undignified, beaten, and pierced for me. For my transgressions. For my iniquities. For my shortcomings. You became sin so that I could become righteous. Pure. White as snow. So that I could have grace.

When I find myself sinning against you, I remind myself of what you've done for me. I don't run away from you but instead, I run towards you. I press into you. Because there's grace. And over time I find myself sinning less against you. I become better. You, my God, make me better.

Thank you for not holding my sins against me but rather paying for them yourself. Thank you for not abandoning me but fighting for me. Thank you for not giving me what I deserve for my sins but rather giving me eternal life through your Son. Thank you for not banning me from your family but adopting me and making me co-heirs with Christ. Thank you for calling me closer even in my sin.

Scripture: Romans 5:8; Romans 6:23; Ephesians 1:5; Ephesians 2:8; 2 Corinthians 5:21

Application: Remember all those times God came close regardless of your mess-ups and sins. Thank Him for the grace He has lavished on you to be able to commune with Him in the midst of sin. The grace He has given you by being close even though you are not holy as He is holy. The grace He has given you by not condemning you when you make the same mistakes, but rather loving you unconditionally. What greater love is there than this?

16

Merciful God

God,

Thank you for your new mercies every day.

Since the beginning of time, you have been merciful. When the Israelites started doubting you and complaining and when their faith failed them, you did not hold their sins against them but rather kept your covenant of love with them.

When I start doubting your timing in regards to your promises, you remind me of how no one who trusts in you shall be put to shame. You remind me how you have appointed time for everything. How one day for you is like a thousand years.

When I start doubting your ability to come through on your promises, you remind me of how you parted the Red Sea. You remind me of how you gave Jericho to your people by marching around the city 7 times without even having to fight. You remind me of how you allowed Sarah and Abraham to bear a child in their old age.

When I start doubting your words and feeling faithless, you remind me that even if I am faithless, you still remain faithful.

For it's in your nature. You remind me that you are the author and perfecter of my faith and how you can do a lot with a mustard seed-sized faith.

When I start pulling away and find my faith failing me, you strengthen me and breathe fresh hope and faith in me. For not even faith is mine to claim. It all comes from you, merciful God.

Scripture: Lamentations 3:22-23; Ecclesiastes 3:1; Genesis 21:1-5; Exodus 14:21-22; Joshua 6:1-20

Application: Think about all the times God has been merciful to you. He does not have to be, but He chooses to. We don't deserve His grace or mercy, but He is that intentional and loving. Friend, stand firm knowing that what He promised, He will do. Stand firm knowing that even if your faith is weak today, if you seek Him, He will breathe fresh hope into it. His promises have never failed and He won't start now. Write down 1-2 promises you are waiting on God for and a standing verse for each one of them.

	Promise	Verse
1.	_____	_____
2.	_____	_____
3.	_____	_____

17

You are My Sustenance

Jesus

I wake up with a cheerful heart because of you
I go about my day expecting you to speak
And I lay down thankful for your whispers meeting me
For you, Jesus, are my sustenance

So speak Lord
I am listening
Whisper in my spirit
The depths of who you are

You Lord, are what keeps my heart going
Knowing that I will see you again, face to face
Knowing that I will hear your sweet voice once again
For you, Jesus, are my sustenance

So speak Lord
I am listening
Paint in my dreams
The mysteries of your heart

Your voice is the only thing that can keep my spirit alive
It's like water to my soul

Melodies to my ears
Sustenance to my body

And every morning I wait expectantly once again
Knowing that you will show me your face
And will let me hear your voice
Thank you Jesus, for being my sustenance

Scripture: Jeremiah 29:13; Jeremiah 33:3; Psalm 29:4; 1 Kings 19:12

Application: How are you living your days? Are you expecting God to speak? Is a new revelation of who He is what gets you excited in your day? Friend, let's not grow comfortable in our relationship with God. If you have forsaken His voice this season and have let the things of this world speak louder than Him, take time to repent. Ask Him to show you how He can sustain you better than fleeting, worldly things.

18

At The Cross

God,

Thank you for the cross. For giving your only Son so we could be close. Jesus, I was the joy set before you on that cross. As you were pierced, beaten, and mocked, you were thinking of me. You were thinking of how worth it I was.

You saw the gold in me even when people did not. You accepted me even before I was rejected. You did not hesitate to sacrifice the best you had in exchange for a relationship with me. So I let that sink in: I was worth it for Jesus, the King of Kings.

This is real love. That you would become human, come to this earth, and die for me. That you would remove all my sins and not hold them against me, but rather give me abundant grace.

So I remind myself how at calvary, you changed my destiny. At calvary, you changed my trajectory. You tore the veil. You opened the door for a relationship. No more religion, only friendship.

Now I can approach Your throne boldly. No second-guessing at hand. No condemnation at play. But rather a humble invitation to be with you. To look at you. To become more like you. And to be transformed by you, my King. I pray my life would be ever so slightly worthy of your sacrifice.

Scripture: Luke 23:26-39

Application: Read the story of the crucifixion of Jesus and ask Him to reveal to you His intention behind it. But most importantly, rejoice in the fact that we can be close to Him! How could we even repay Him? The good news is that we don't have to and we would never be able to. So we get to just soak it in and enjoy Him.

19

Who Am I to Question You?

God,

Who am I to doubt your words over me?
Who am I to know what is best for me?
Who am I to doubt your ability to come through for me?

You Lord, know the end from the beginning
You Lord, predestined me in my mother's womb
You Lord, prepared good works for me to walk into

Who am I to question your ways?
Who am I to rationalize my life?
Who am I to think I know better than the Holy One?

You Lord, have endless thoughts concerning me
You Lord, made me beautifully and wonderfully
You Lord, have engrafted me in the palm of your hand

My life Lord is a miracle in itself
The fact that you picked me is a wonder alone
The fact that you love me in my weakness amazes me every day

I am merely the clay and you are the potter
So I choose to not question Your molding abilities

I choose to accept how You've showed up in my life
I choose to delight in You

Thank you, my King.

Scripture: Psalm 139; Isaiah 29:16

Application: I used to struggle accepting myself -- my personality, appearance, and quirks. I did not understand why I couldn't be "normal" like other people. I also used to think I did not matter or was significant. But then God gave me a revelation of who He created me to be. And friend, this goes for you as well. You were intricately made by and for Jesus. He does not make mistakes. He only makes masterpieces. So friend, in what area are you struggling to accept yourself? In what areas do you think you know better than God? Today, I encourage you to trust in the potter. He is intentional with what He makes. And He wants to show you His mysteries for your life today. Simply ask Him.

20

In The Process

God,

Thank you for giving me a promise and being gracious enough to prepare me for it. Thank you for walking me through the process. For being so near in the middle. In the waiting. In the unknown. For guiding me through the uncertainty.

Thank you that when I feel antsy to give you all and step into my calling, you meet me and quiet my soul. When I am dreading my work week and would prefer to weep at your feet, you remind me that you are closer than a brother. When I would prefer to worship and serve you all day, you remind me that there is an appointed time for everything.

Thank you for shifting my perspective and showing me how serving, loving, and encouraging others, even at work, is serving you. Thank you for showing me it's not about me, but about you. Thank you for revealing to me how losing my life is finding it. Thank you for opening my eyes on how you can use me even in the mundane.

In the meantime, I will praise you. I will serve you by serving others. By being kind to others. By being a bright light. I will remind myself of how David served over 20 years before stepping into what you had made him for. And I will remind my soul that what you have spoken over me will come to pass. Thank you for being a good Father who guides me in the process.

Scripture: Psalm 131:1-2, Matthew 10:39; 2 Samuel 5:4

Application: I wrote this in a season where I wanted to jump into what the Lord has called me to do even though it was not the time yet. I have learned that in those moments, in the process, God is the closest. He is molding our hearts and fertilizing them so we can bear good fruit. So think about the promises God has given you. How has He prepared you for them? What did the process look like? Or if you are in the middle, what is He teaching you? You see, David had to wait 20 years between being anointed to be king and being appointed King. Friend, our times are not His times. So I encourage you today to take heart and trust in the Lord. He will renew your strength until due time.

21

I Surrender: All Is For You

God,

Thank you for choosing me. Little ole me. Fearful me. Faithless me. Thank you for setting me apart for your glory. For your wonders.

Thank you for stretching your mighty arm towards me. Thank you for believing in me. Thank you for seeing my strength in the midst of my weakness. Thank you for speaking life to me when every flower in the garden of my heart was withering away. You truly give beauty for ashes.

What is impossible to you Lord if I surrender my life to you? You turn my mourning into dancing. My sorrows into rejoicing. My cares into testimonies. My anxiety into peace. My fears into faith.

So I surrender. Everything. My preconceived ideas of you. My dreams and aspirations. My timeline. My will. Let it be a living sacrifice to you, Lord. And as I give it all to you, let it all be used for your glory. All the pain. All the hurt. All the successes. The mountains and the valleys. Everything my King.

Scripture: Romans 12:1-2, Psalm 30:11-12, Isaiah 61:3

Application: Most of my life I wanted to control everything. My timeline, my life, and the outcome of things. But I've learned that letting go of control does not mean things won't happen. It just means God has a better plan and/or something better. So I ask you, what are you holding on to that God wants you to give up? Will you surrender your desires and dreams and let God surprise you with His best? He never disappoints. You see, just as Jesus was prophesied to give Israel beauty for ashes in Isaiah 61:3, so He can do the same for you. You see, in the Old Testament, when individuals were mourning, they would place ashes on their heads. On the other hand, oil was a symbol of celebration and joy. Would you let Him remove those ashes from your head and cover you with His oil of gladness and joy?

22

History

Jesus,

I love our history. Our moments together. Our memories. Our hours shared. Every second enjoyed in your presence. I never want to forget them. I never want to hold them loosely. I never want to take them for granted. For my history with you, LORD is the only thing that can't be taken away from me. It's my testimony.

All those moments you came near — whether to love, encourage or exhort me — those made our history Lord. And it goes deep. It's not a one-time thing. It's not a waste of time. Rather it's everlasting, it's magical, and it's sweet. And even though it's not perfect and sometimes even messy, I wouldn't change a thing.

So my soul cries out to you. It longs for you. And it demands for more history to be made. It can't help but spend more time with you. It can't help but see you face to face. It can't help but imagine a future with you. And to behold your amazing grace. Because apart from you I have no good thing.

So thank you for showing up every time. Thank you for the history you have already planned next — our present and our future. I pray that it will be filled with your ever-lasting presence and love. I promise to never forsake those times but to cherish them fully, my King.

Scripture: Psalm 84; Psalm 16:2

Application: What a blessing to be able to commune with God wherever we are through His Holy Spirit. He is accessible 24/7! In the Old Testament, individuals could only get close to God by being near the temple, where the Arc of the Covenant was. Friend, make it a priority today to remember all the times God has met you. He did not have to but He chose to. Give Him thanks for being so intentional! Thank Him for making history with you! Thank Him for the testimony in your life and ask Him for more! Now, turn to Psalm 84 and ask God to give you that same zeal to want to be in His courts/presence as the psalmist. Thank Him for all the history that was made even when you were passing through your own "Valley of Baka." You see, even in the hard times, we get to make sweet memories with Him by our side.

23

Lifter of My Burdens

God,

When everything seems to be going wrong. When I fear picking up the phone due to fear of bad news. When I feel anxiety creeping into my soul and my heart due to my circumstances. When I can't bear the thought of having another burden to carry on my own.

I remind myself, that you are my ever-present help in trouble. I remind myself, that you are my strength and my shield. I remind myself that when I place my trust in you, you help me. I remind myself, that your yoke is easy and your burden is light.

And once I remember that you don't walk away in the hard times, but rather come in close, my heartbeat quiets down. My soul steadies. My mind declutters. My stress subsides.

And my lips start praising your name. I start removing the heavy bags from my shoulders and you are faithful to place them on yourself — the One who died for them already.

And all of a sudden, I can breathe again. I can lie in peace and be okay with being a fragile human who gets to depend on

You. I exhale my problems out and inhale your presence — full of your peace. And it's all good again. Thank you, lifter of my burdens. Prince of Peace.

Scripture: Psalm 46:1; Matthew 11:28-30; Psalm 28:7; Isaiah 9:6

Application: Are you full of burdens? Are you tired of having to "deal" and carry" them all by yourself? Are you exhausted from having to come up with solutions to difficult situations? Friend, you don't have to carry those burdens. You don't have to do life on your own. Jesus is with you and He lives in you through the Holy Spirit! And let me remind you that He is the Prince of Peace, the Wonderful Counselor, and the lifter of your head. So whatever burdens you are carrying, I invite you to release them to Him. He will not disappoint you.

24

What Can I Do For You?

Jesus,

What can I do for you? Show me the way to your heart. Is it through songs? Is it through dance? Is it through soaking in your presence? Is it through my life? I know it's not enough, but it's what I have.

What is it that moves you, my King? I can cry these tears, sing these songs, write these prayers, or delight in you, but it all seems insufficient. It all seems unworthy of who you are and what you've done.

What is it that pulls your heartstrings, my King? In the midst of all I hear you say over me "Choosing to spend time with me is what moves me." I pray that I would make it my life to choose the better thing: being with you my King Jesus.

Help me be a Mary in this Martha-world. Help me choose you instead of the busyness of this world. Help me understand how my time with you means more to you than the time I put in achievements and titles. Help me choose the better thing rather than the worldly and popular thing.

Scripture: Luke 10:38-42; Psalm 84:10

Application: I believe there is nothing more we can do for God to love us more, but I do know He delights when His children love Him. So, how can you love Jesus today? What decisions are you making to allow you to spend time with Him? What are you saying no to so you can say yes to Him? Write down 3 ways you will be more intentional to spend time with your Father below.

1.

2.

3.

25

You Call Me as I Am

God,

You don't wait for me to be perfect to pull me closer
You don't wait for me to get it right to call me higher
You love me as I am
And you call me as I am

Thank you for seeing me rightly
Thank you for accepting me as I am
Sinful and broken
Lost but now found

Thank you for patience in the refinement
For not giving up on me in the process, but rather cheering
me on
For not expecting perfection, but rather extending me grace
You are full of mercy and love

Thank you for not only calling the equipped,
But equipping the called
Thank you for using me in my weakness
Even in my worst days

For you use the foolish things of the world
To shame the wise
You use the weak to show your strength
You call the last to be the first

Thank you for your upside-down Kingdom
Thank you for calling me as I am

Scripture: 1 Corinthians 1:27; 2 Corinthians 12:9;
Isaiah 40:29

Application: I've always been humbled by how God has called me to serve, follow, and be in relationship with Him. I am a sinner, have flaws, and definitely appear foolish to the world. But that is what I love about our God, He calls the most unlikely people and still believes and has faith in us. He is patient in our refinement and does not hold our sins against us. Instead, He calls us to boast in our weaknesses so His power may rest on us. Today, thank God for choosing you to impact others and to be in relationship with Him. There is no greater privilege.

26

The Chambers of My Heart

God,

You deserve all the chambers of my heart
All the spaces — big or small, healed or wounded
Even the cracks left from lesser lovers,
You desire them

So I give them back to you
The only one who can heal them
The only one who can satisfy them
The only one who can make them new again

I'm sorry for the times I contaminated my heart
For the times unworthy thoughts took hold of it
For the times I allowed lesser lovers to take residence in it
For the times dissatisfaction planted roots of bitterness in it

So I give you permission to cut every branch that does not bear
fruit
So that I may remain in you
I give you permission to prune the branches that do bear fruit
So that they may be more fruitful

I give you permission to groom the garden of my heart
Remove any weeds that are preventing life from flourishing
Plant seeds of your love and peace
I just want your presence and nature living in me

Conquer my heart again, my King

Scripture: John 15; Psalm 139:23-24; Psalm 51:10; Hebrews 12:15

Application: Sometimes we harbor roots of bitterness, unforgiveness, and envy in our hearts which prevent us from living the life God intended for us to have. So today, make it a priority to examine your heart and most importantly, allow God to search you. Friend, have you allowed God into every chamber? Is He Lord of your heart? Have you allowed Him to conquer it? Pray for God to expose any areas where you have not let Him in and ask Him to walk you through His healing process.

27

You Filled In the Gap

Jesus,

At the cross
When your blood was shed,
You filled in the empty space
You filled in the gap

The empty space that separated us
That sin that made us distant
Just so you could live in me,
You filled in the gap

And now I am righteous in front of the Father
I can lock eyes with Him with no shame
And I can come boldly to His throne
Without condemnation or rejection

Oh how sweet what you've done for me
Becoming human and experiencing temptation
Not giving into it but rather
Giving up your life to stand in the middle

How precious is this good news
You filled the gap

You tore the veil
You finished it

Scripture: 2 Philippians 2:5-8; Hebrews 4:15;
1 Timothy 2:5; Matthew 27:50-51

Application: Have you ever pondered on the fact that God so loved you that He was willing to come into Earth as an innocent and fragile baby to save us from sin and death? He willingly chose to lay down his comfort as God and become a mere human, experience temptation and every emotion we have ever felt. All for you. To be close to you. I pray that truth never becomes common for us. Today, thank Him for His sacrifice, for cleansing you of your sins, and for choosing discomfort over comfort. Just for you.

28

You're the One Thing

God,

Earnestly I seek you. Earnestly I desire you. Not for what you can provide for me. Not for how you can bless me. Not for your riches or abundance. But for who you are. For your nature. For your presence. For your affections. So I remind my soul how your love is better than life. And I declare that my lips will forever glorify you.

I choose to slow down. To let the world pause around me. And to look at you. To take you in. And to tell you how I want to sing songs to you. How I want to offer you a sacrifice of praise. How I want to bless you. How I want to please you — just you my Jesus. Let my songs pierce your heart. Let my words move you.

For you're the One thing worth striving for. You're the One thing worth pressing in for. You're the One thing worth running to. It's you my Jesus. My one and only, You.

Scripture: Hebrews 13:15: Psalm 63:1-3

Application: Is God your one and only thing? Is He the most important person in your life? You see, regardless of the answer, He still wants a relationship with you. So I invite you to set intentional time to spend with Him today, this week, this month. These will be the most precious and life-changing moments of your life.

29

My Hiding Place

Jesus,

You are my hiding place.

When my heart starts being gripped by fear of the unknown, when trouble comes, when the situation seems to be escalating — You Jesus, are my hiding place.

When I feel hopeless, when everyone starts speaking fear over my life, when there seems to be no safe place around me — You Jesus, are my hiding place.

I let the words and fears of this world ungrip my heart and I enter my hiding place — Your sweet presence. There, you sing songs of deliverance over me. You hide me under the shadow of your wings. And even though it seems like I am surrounded by darkness, I am secure. For your rod and your staff, they comfort me.

And in my hiding place, Your word promises me to guide me and instruct me in the way I should go. You Jesus, lock eyes with me and counsel me. You train my hands for war, my fingers for battle. You give me a shield to protect my mind and body- Your faithfulness. So I choose to trust you Jesus, my Prince of Peace. My compass. My Mighty Warrior.

Scripture: Psalm 32:7-8, Psalm 91; Psalm 144:1

Application: I wrote this during the COVID-19 crisis. In the midst of a world gripped by fear, God spoke to me about how He is our hiding place even when we are surrounded by darkness and chaos. So today ask yourself, what situation or narrative am I allowing to steal my peace and prevent me from trusting in God? Let God show you how He is your hiding place in your time of trouble and bring to remembrance situations in which He has come through in your life. May we never let this word rob us of what Jesus already died for, Heavenly peace.

30

You Accept Me

Jesus,

Around and around I go, looking to be loved for who I am. Trying to be found by a man who understands and loves me not for my looks but my heart. Trying to make it happen on my own strength. Getting frustrated, disappointed, and hurt — wondering if that person even exists.

But when I lock eyes with you, Jesus, I remember who I am. I am not someone's choice. I am not someone's option. I am not someone's rejection. I am not like everyone else. I am not common. But I am set apart. Before the foundations of the Earth, you separated me from the rest of the world. Like a lily among thorns. You breathed life on me and called me out — to be yours first and then someone else's.

And you have said over me that I am extravagant. That I am your special possession. That your plans for me are good and not evil — to bring me hope and a future. That you have that man who will be like an apple tree among the trees of the forest. A man who offers the shade of protection and the fruit that is so sweet to my taste.

So I quiet my soul. I let faith rise up. I do not concern myself with things too lofty for me, but rather I trust in your ultimate word: that those who delight themselves in the Lord will be given the desires of their heart. So thank you, Jesus. Thank you for accepting me for who I am and for creating that man who will love me like you love the church. Thank you for having an appointed time for my future.

Scripture: Ephesians 1:14, Song of Songs 2:2; 1 Peter 2:9; Jeremiah 29:11; Psalm 131; Ephesians 5:25

Application: I wrote this during my single season. I was feeling hopeless and tired of being disappointed in the dating process. But what I loved the most during those times was how God met me. He came near and reminded me of who I was and how He saw me. So I encourage you, remember how Jesus met you when you thought a desire and dream was too impossible for Him. Remember how He came through and praise Him in the waiting room of your next desire.

31

Brightest Jewel

Jesus,

I want to be your brightest jewel.

Thank you for loving me unconditionally. Thank you for searching my heart and finding the fault in me to call me higher. Thank you for creating in me a clean heart — set apart for you.

Thank you for being a jealous God who wants my whole heart, not just pieces of it. Thank you for convicting me when I allow lesser lovers to invade parts of my heart that belong to you.

My Jesus, help me be all yours. Help me have my eyes only fixed on you. Help me find no greater love than you. Help me want to please you more than the world. Help the words of my mouth and the meditations of my heart be pleasing to you.

My Lord. Out of all your jewels, I want to be your brightest jewel. I want to be the one who stands out the most to you. I want to be your most treasured possession. I want to be your most valuable asset.

I want to be your brightest jewel.

Scripture: Psalm 51:10; Exodus 34:14; Psalm 19:14

Application: All my life I have always wanted to please God so this prayer is a frequent one for me. If you are reading this I believe you also have this desire. So join me as ask God to search and convict you of any wrong ways. Ask Him to purify your heart. Finally, what can you do today to please Him and find favor with Him? But not out of a place of religion, but out of love for Him.

32

What Are Humans?

Jesus,

Thank you for humbling yourself by stooping down to Earth into a human body. All for love. To remove the veil that separated us. Thank you for fighting the darkness of legalism and sin to have a relationship with us.

What kind of God are you that you concern yourself with us humans? What kind of God are you that you would have endless thoughts concerning our well being? What kind of God are you that you would care when we grieve? To the point of collecting our tears in a bottle?

But you God, you knew our frame before you chose us — pure dust. You, God, knew how our human life is like a temporary mist that vanishes in your appointed time. You, God, knew how we are like the grass of the Earth — easily blown by the wind and easily forgotten.

Help us understand how you, Almighty God, would leave all your power to fight sin and death to have all of our hearts. What kind of God would willingly inhabit our sinless bodies?

Jesus, help us see the magnitude of your sacrifice. Help us see how we are nothing without you. Help us realize that we can only keep going because you strengthen us. Help us realize how you are our most prized possession.

Scripture: Matthew 27:51, Psalm 139:17; Psalm 8:4; James 4:14; Psalm 103:14-16

Application: Ponder on the mercy and lovingkindness of our God, who sent His only Son to die for us to be able to have a relationship with us, mere humans. He could have vanished us all for all the time we have forsaken Him and had other idols, but He continues to choose us in the midst of our rebellion. Thank God for His sacrifice and let it sink deep in your heart — without Him we are nothing.

33

You Are Faithful

Jesus,

When I look at you,
I remember how great is your faithfulness
When I gaze upon you,
I see the rider who is called faithful and true

And it hits me
It does not matter what my life looks like
It does not matter what my circumstances say
Because you Jesus, remain faithful

What you have said will come to pass
Your words are weighty and true
And they never return void
But rather they bear fruit

Therefore, I will not waver in unbelief
Regarding the promises you have made
For you who promised are faithful
And continue to be throughout all generations

Therefore, I will not concern myself
With things too lofty for me to understand

For you keep your covenant of love
To a thousand generations of those who trust in you

Scripture: Lamentations 3:23; Revelation 19:11; Isaiah 55:11; Romans 4:20-21; Psalm 119:90; Psalm 131

Application: Have you ever been faithless? Have you ever had a time when you were too discouraged to put your hope in God due to fear of being disappointed? Friend, the best way to build up our faith is to bring to remembrance all those times God has been faithful! About 2 years ago I started a book of remembrance where I write all the ways and times God has come true in His promises and word. I encouraged you, start a book of remembrance and keep a record of God's faithfulness to build your faith later on! And remember, not one of His promises has ever failed and He will not start with you.

34

Thank You

God,

Thank you for choosing me. Before I knew you, you had knitted me together in my mother's womb. Before I was even born, you had a purpose and a destiny for me. Before the foundation of the earth, you knew me. Thank you for the gift of life with you.

Thank you for incessantly knocking at the door of my heart, even when I seemed cold towards you. Thank you for not giving up on me, but rather moving closer to me. Thank you for lingering even when I seemed not to care — when I seemed indifferent.

And when I was done living in my own strength. When I was done trying to figure everything out. When I was done living for myself, you were right there. With open hands. No shame at hand. No condemnation in sight. Simply with an invitation, of unconditional love.

God, saying yes to you surpasses any decision of my life. Thank you for letting me be so close in the midst of my sin. In the midst of the deceitfulness of my heart. In the midst of my pride.

Thank you, my King.

Scripture: Psalms 139:13; Jeremiah 1:5; Revelations 3:20; Luke 15:20

Application: I grew up in a Christian home and was surrounded by church and prayerful parents. Somewhere along the way, I became indifferent towards God. I still had a relationship with Him but sometimes pride got in the way. Even in the midst of that, He still chose me. He still loved me. He still guarded me. So ask yourself this question: How was your life before knowing Jesus and how did He leave the 99 to find you, the one? How can you thank Him today for His love and relentless pursuit of you?

35

I Love to Love You

Jesus,

What greater privilege do I have but to love you
What greater joy than to sit at your feet
To feel your presence surrounding me
I just love to love you

What greater honor than to steward your presence
What greater joy than to hear you speak over me
With your tender voice full of mercy
I just love to love you

For when I am intentional to gaze upon you
You come close — closer than a brother
So near — nearer than my skin
And you speak tenderly to me

And I become lovesick
For your love is better than life
It's richer than any banquet I could feast on
Indeed, your presence is the banquet

Thank you for letting me love you, my King
Thank you for letting me feast on you, my King

Scripture: Psalm 63

Application: Every time I go to Jesus' feet, I get filled up. I get encouraged. I become satisfied. And I realized that every time I love Him, my spirit rejoices. Friend, we were made to love Him. We were made to worship Him. He is the only thing that can satisfy your being. So I ask you, how are you loving God today? Make time to commune with Him today and let Him delight in you.

36

Let Me Keep Burning

God,

Since the beginning of creation, you knew me
And your plans for me were good
I was made for and unto you Lord
To love you and worship you, forever

So let my heart keep burning for you
Don't let the oil of my lamp run dry on you
Don't let the beats of my heart be for someone else but you
I want to keep burning for you, you alone

So I allow you to invade my heart, even the ugly parts
Knowing that you don't run away when it gets messy
But rather press in closer
And come through with fresh oil every time

So let my heart keep burning for you
Don't allow a moment to pass where I don't give you all I have
Don't let me harden my heart and forsake your presence
I want to keep burning for you, you alone

Let my heart remain expectant
To hear your voice, feel your presence

Let my heart be child-like in faith
Full of wonder and joy

I want to keep burning for you
You alone

Scripture: Jeremiah 29:11; Romans 11:36; Matthew 25

Application: Are you burning for God alone? You see, God is a jealous God and wants *all* of your heart. Turn to Exodus 34:10-14. Here we see how God was making a covenant with the Israelites at Mount Sinai and reveals another part of His nature, one of His names, Qanna. This Hebrew word translates to Jealous and is related to a marriage relationship between Israel and God. Since we have been grafted into the Kingdom of God, this also applies to us! So friend, let's make it a priority today to be intentional about stewarding our relationship with the Lord and be like the wise virgins in Matthew 25 who had enough oil for their bridegroom's return.

37

Heavenly Places

God,

Thank you for chasing us down when we were living in our flesh. Thank you for not letting the sin in us separate us from you. Thank you for not casting us out of your presence but rather allowing us to be seated with you in heavenly places.

Remind us how we have been grafted into your family and with that, have been given all dominion over all the earth. Remind us that you have given us the authority to bind and loose things on earth as they are in Heaven. Remind us that the power of life and death lies in our tongue.

And even though you are a sovereign God who does not need our human help, you still choose to use us. You still want our help, our input. So we ask you, reveal to us your plans for the earth so we can partner with you. Help us burn for what your heart desires. Help us take our right standing and help us be bold in your kingdom. Help us speak forth what we do not see. Help us bring heaven on earth.

> **Scripture**: Ephesians 2:1-7; Genesis 1:26; Matthew 18:18

Application: Have you ever thought how we are seated in heavenly places with Christ? In the midst of our sinful nature, God still wanted us to be part of His story. He gave us dominion over the Earth and gave us authority in our tongue! Friend, even though He is sovereign, He wants us to partner with Him to bring Heaven on Earth. How humbling is that? So today, make sure to attune your ear to His voice and ask Him how you can partner today to declare what He wants to see on Earth.

38

You Are Intoxicating

Jesus,

You are intoxicating. Every time you come in and walk into the room, your being captivates me. Your presence cannot be taken lightly. It cannot be overshadowed. It cannot be overcome. For you are the radiance of the glory of God.

You are intoxicating. No matter what I am doing, as soon as I feel your Spirit, I fall at your feet. No second thought at hand. For You are seated at the right hand of Almighty God, yet you are not full of pride or arrogance. Rather, you draw me in with your unfailing love. Full of humility. Full of purity. Full of delight. So I drink your love for it surely satisfies.

You are intoxicating. So much that I can recognize your fragrance anytime — a pleasing aroma to me. For you are my beloved — radiant and outstanding among ten thousand. Altogether lovely, altogether one of a kind. For you are like an apple tree among the forest — refreshing to the taste but hard to find another like it.

You are indeed intoxicating.

Scripture: Song of Songs; Hebrews 1:3; Jeremiah 31:3

Application: How precious and intoxicating is God's presence! Think about all the times God has met you and start thanking Him for it! He does not have to come but He chooses to out of His lovingkindness. If you are reading this, He is inviting you to have a Song of Songs relationship with Him -- where He becomes your ultimate desire and sustenance. Pray that God starts revealing Himself to you in such a way and make sure to dive into the book of Song of Songs to start this journey.

39

Will It Be Worth It?

Jesus,

Will my sacrifices be worth it in the end? Will the things of this world and the pleasures which I have rejected pay off in the end? Will the peer pressure I've endured, the negative comments, the social gathering I've blown off to spend time with you be worth it in the end? Show me a glimpse, give me a peek, a taste of what's to come. Help me sustain my faith for the promises you've given me — the things to come.

And I felt you saying over me: *My child, when you feel like you need a peek, a glimpse, or a taste of what's coming, remember that I am your hope of glory. Remember that because I live in you, you can hope again — without needing to actually see what's coming. Remember that the things of this world are horrible masters but beautiful gifts from me. But I am all that your soul really needs in the end — pure living water, the bread of life. For you were created by, for and unto Me.*

What is success if you are not completely mine? What is marriage if you are not already married to me? What are children if you don't have child-like faith?

Jesus, thank you for always meeting me Lord. I surrender my desires, expectations, and entitlement. I'm done painting pictures of what I want and acting as if I need anything else from you, for you know what I need and ultimately you are all I need. Your presence and your words are the only tastes and glimpses I need — my hope of glory.

Scripture: Colossians 1:27; 2 Corinthians 5:7; Matthew 6:24; John 4:14; John 6:35

Application: God has promised us many gifts in His word, but when we desire them more than Him we are making them our master. God is the only one that should have all our hearts. Think about the desires of your heart and ask the Lord to show you if you are placing them above Him. God desires to have the first place in our hearts so He can be our hope of glory and we can have faith in His promises -- without requiring Him to reveal when and how things will come. So let's make it our goal to walk by faith and not by sight today.

40

You Are My Help

God,

Thank you for being my help. Thank you for not forsaking me in the time of trouble. Thank you for coming so near — closer than the wind blowing on my hair. Even before I cry out to You, You are attentive to my prayers. For you do not slumber or sleep on me — You watch my every move. You consider everything I do.

And soon as you hear my cry for help, You come. For you are where my help comes from. You are my ever-present help in trouble. You watch over my coming and my going and You concern yourself with the steps I take. Though I might stumble, I will surely not fall — for you Lord uphold me with your hand.

And as soon as You come I can sense your presence. You wrap Your mighty but comforting arms around me, like a shield against my troubles. And you reach down into the deep waters of my troubles that drowned me and rescue me — my mighty savior.

And when I wonder why you would save *me*. You remind me that you delight in me — in whom you are well pleased in. So when I am hopeless, I wait in hope for You my God, for You are my help and my shield.

Scripture: Psalm 121; Psalm 33:14-21; Psalm 34:15, Psalm 46:1; Psalm 37:23-24; Psalm 18:16-19

Application: Read and meditate on Psalm 121. This psalm was written by the psalmist to ask God for protection and remind himself that God will never leave him- especially in the time of trouble. He reminds us how God never falls asleep watching over His children, but rather, is vigilant and is watching our every step. Friend, what troubles are you going through today? Let me remind you that there are no surprises for your God. He never slumbers watching over you and He responds to your cry for help. So today, pray this psalm back to Him and remind your spirit of how good of a protector He is.

41

My Righteousness

Jesus,

When I feel like I have been relying on my own strength and capabilities, when I feel like I am good enough on my own, when I let roots of self-righteousness be planted in my heart, remind me that I am who I am because of your great mercy and love. Remind me that I have come this far because of your lovingkindness.

So forgive me Lord for putting the glory on myself rather than on You, my hope of glory. Forgive me for exalting my own flesh instead of the grace You have extended towards me. I give you permission to humble me and remind me that you are the only righteous one.

Thank you for being slow to anger and abounding in love. Thank you for not treating me as my sins deserve, but rather being compassionate and gracious. So I thank you Jesus, for not holding my sins against me. Thank you that as far as the east is from the west, so far have you removed my transgressions from me.

Remind me that the only reason I can be righteous before you is because of your sacrifice. Because of you Jesus, I am in right standing with the Father. Because of you my Jesus, I don't have to be perfect -- I can come with my mess and still have an audience of one with my God. Thank you. May I forever boast on you my King, my only righteousness. Jehovah Tsidkanu.

Scripture: Psalm 103:8-14; Romans 3:9-10; Romans 3:22

Application: Have you ever felt like you were relying on your own strength? Have you ever felt like you deserve a certain thing due to how "good" you are? If you have, repent and ask God for forgiveness. He is the only perfect and righteous one. Even in the Old Testament, God is called *Jehovah Tsidkanu* which translates to, "The Lord Who is our Righteousness." You see, we are only righteous through our faith in Jesus Christ. And that my friend, is good news.

42

Is This What it Looks Like?

Jesus,

Is this what it looks like to be in love?
To want to gaze upon your beauty all the days of my life?
To want to spend time with you instead of the pleasures of this world?
To be fully satisfied by your presence instead of the richest of meals?

Those around me might not understand
They might think I'm exaggerating
They might think I'm crazy
But I have tasted and I have seen that you are good

Is this what it looks like to be in love?
To look at the Heavens and see you?
To feel the wind blowing against my cheek and feel you?
To hear raindrops against my window and be reminded of you?

Those close to me might not understand
But you have chosen me before the foundation of the Earth
You have drawn me in with unfailing kindness
You Lord, have set me apart —for your delight

So I don't fight it
I don't resist it
I don't try to make sense of it
I don't excuse it

Rather, I soak it all up
I let go of my inhibitions
I let it intoxicate me
I allow myself to fall more in love with you

And I choose to see you in everything

Scripture: Psalm 27:4; Psalm 34:8; Ephesians 1:4; Jeremiah 31:3; Galatians 1:15

Application: Friend, do you know what God set you apart before the foundations of the Earth? He chose to draw you in with His unfailing love to be captivated by Him. We were made to look, worship, and fall in love with Him all the days of our lives. So ask yourself today, "Am I more in love with the things of this world or with the One true thing, Jesus?" Have you let Him captivate and pursue you? I encourage you, ask Him to do so today, and let yourself see Him in the smallest of things.

43

The Desert

Jesus,

When I was relying on my own strength
Trying to find my worth in worldly things
Living for myself and running to lesser lovers
Without finding satisfaction in my soul

You reached out — out of love
You lead me into the wilderness
And turned me into a parched land
You made me a desert

You stripped me from my idols
None left in sight
Even if I chased for them I did not reach them
Even if I looked for them I could not find them

And it was only you and I
I learned to rely on you
You became my source
You became my sustenance

In the desert, you purified me — white as snow
In the desert, you refined me — shiny as a diamond

In the desert, you circumcised my heart — like the Israelites
And you removed the names of lesser lovers from my lips

For you made a covenant with me
You betrothed me to yourself for eternity
You bewedded me
With love and mercy

No longer do I concern myself with the things of this world
For all I desire is your presence
All I desire is to please you
My God, my Father, my Husband

Scripture: Hosea; Song of Songs

Application: Read the Book of Hosea, especially chapter 2. This book paints a picture of how God judged and punished Israel, due to having lesser lovers, to the point of alluring her to the desert. Out of mercy and love, He brings Israel to her knees so she can knock at mercy's door and find the One true God, where the joy is really at. He depicts this through a marriage relationship between Hosea and Gomer, a prostitute. Friend, ask yourself, am I truly and faithfully married to King Jesus, or am I finding satisfaction in lesser things? Take time and ask God to reveal any object, relationship, or status you are placing above Him. You see, He is a jealous God and wants all your heart.

44

Take Me Back to the Beginning

God,

I might be by myself, but I am not alone
I might be on my own, but I feel you so close
You never left, but rather you drew near
You never abandoned me, but rather you encamped around me

And you remind me how it's always been like this,
But I was too distracted to see
You've always been speaking,
But my soul was too uneasy to listen

Take me back to the beginning,
Where you were the center of my life
Take me back to the beginning,
Where you were the most important thing in sight

So I do not forsake this moment
When it's you and I alone
When you removed my busyness
So I could behold the only one true God

Thank you for caring enough to stop the world for me
Thank you for reminding me that you are where life really is

Let me never take you for granted my Jesus
For you are all I ever wanted

Take me back to the beginning

Scripture: Hebrews 13:8

Application: Remember when COVID-19 hit in 2020 and how everyone's world changed? Gatherings ceased, work decreased, idols were removed, and busyness slowed down. We were all forced to recognize what had been constant all along, the One true God. The one who has never changed. The alpha and the omega. The one that knows the end from the beginning. Take time to reflect on how God met you in that season. What benefits have you reaped from that encounter?

45

I Want the Real Thing

God,

I'm done giving into the fleeting emotions of my heart. I'm done being moved and tossed by the waves of doubt and unbelief. I've had enough of giving into the temporary pleasures of this world. I'm ready for you alone.

I want the real thing.
The source of living water.

So I give you permission to shift my affections towards you. I give you permission to take all of my heart. And I give you permission to make all my thoughts about you alone.

I want the real thing.
The bread of life.

I don't want to strive any more for what I think I need. I don't want to beg for affection. I don't want to live thinking that I have to earn acceptance. Remind me that with you, I have rest, affection, and acceptance — the unconditional and everlasting ones.

I want the real thing.
The One who satisfies.

So I surrender — my thoughts, my emotions, my desires, my life, my preconceived ideas of when things should happen. I hold them loosely and hold you tightly — the one real thing.

Scripture: James 1:6; John 4:14; John 6:35; Isaiah 58:11

Application: I wrote this prayer during a season where I was giving into my emotions instead of what God had promised. A season where I was leaning more on what I saw than on what God's word said. So I ask you, where are you putting your trust today? Are you trusting in fleeting emotions and the physical realm or God's word? And remember, no matter what your promise or desire is, their fulfillment will never compare to the satisfaction that comes from God alone — the living water and bread of life. So ask Him to shift your perspective and to reveal Himself as the only One who satisfies.

46

I Trust Your Leadership

God,

I trust your leadership in my life
I don't have to question your design
I don't have to cling to what's not mine
I can just trust you are right by my side

You counsel me with your loving eye
Even at night, you instruct me
You've promised I'd hear your voice
Telling me the way that I should go

You are the Good Shepherd
Who lays down His life for us sheep
Always leading the way
And never leading us astray

You guide me in truth and teach me
You pour down your wisdom and truth
You make me lie down in green pasture
And make me find rest in you

Scripture: Psalm 32:8; Psalm 23:1-3; Psalm 16:7-11; John 10:11-18

Application: We all have hard decisions to make, and sometimes we feel like we can't trust God with them. We feel like we know better. We don't trust His timing. We feel like He does not fully understand therefore we can't trust Him. But friend, today, I want to encourage you to meditate on the scriptures of the day and let them sink in into your heart. You see, God is your Jehovah Raah, your Good Shepherd, which in Hebrew also translates to best friend. You can be yourself with Him! He does know you well and if you let Him, He will Shepherd you into making the best decision.

47

You Are My Everything

Jesus,

When I rise I wait for you to whisper my name
When I go about my day I am expectant to hear your still small voice
When I lay down you are my last and most precious thought
For you, Jesus, are my everything

So if I sing, let every note exalt you
If I write, let every word be about you
If I dance, let every move be for you
For you, Jesus, are my everything

There is nothing or no one greater than You
There is no other person who I would give my whole heart to
There is no other name I would exalt and worship more than yours
For you, Jesus, are my everything

So if I need encouragement, let it come from Your word
If I need affection, let it be from the tenderness of your presence
If I need company, let it be your sweet Spirit
For you, Jesus, are my everything

May I never forsake your presence
May you forever be the center of my life
May I forever love you, with all my heart
For you are worthy of more than just my affections, my King

Scripture: Philippians 3:8-9; Psalm 73:25-26

Application: Is God your everything in this season? Is He the reason why you wake up? If not, ask the Lord to bring you back to that first love – to the beginning of your relationship when you could not wait to talk and commune with Him. Give Him permission to become everything in your life again for everything else does not compare to the joy of being completely His.

48

You Love Me When I'm Unlovable

Jesus,

When my heart fails to trust you and I'm filled with anxiety
When I start doubting your promises and act on my own strength
When I fail to submit my will to you, thinking my ways are higher
I thank you for loving me, even when I'm unlovable

In the midst of all
You still call me by name
You still wrap your arms around me
And you accept me even when others would reject me

You remind me of how proud you are of me
You remind me of how much you love me, no matter my actions
You remind me of how you would leave the 99 for me, the one
I thank you for loving me, even when I'm unlovable

You keep coming every time
You never leave or forsake me
You are constant and faithful
And you speak life into me

And when I feel like I disappointed you,
You remind me how I have always been your first choice

You've never had a second option
You've never had a plan B

So thank you. For still choosing and loving me when I'm unlovable, my King.

Scripture: Luke 15:4; Luke 5:30-31; Deuteronomy 31:6

Application: Yes, we have all sinned and fell short of the glory of God, but the good news is that Jesus came for us, sinners. He came to make us righteous, holy, spotless, and engraft us into God's family. So if you are feeling unlovable, remember that He is willing to leave the other sheep for you — to chase you, embrace you, and love you with an everlasting love.

49

Make Me A Pure Container

God,

Captivate my gaze
Pierce my heart
Remove all contaminants
And fill me with your Spirit

Make me a pure container
A gold and silver utensil
Refined by your truth
And sensible to your presence

Purify me until I am clean
Don't let me settle for where I've been
Set me apart for your glory
So I can be part of your story

A bride lovesick for her King
Weeping at His feet
Wasting her life on Him
And longing to be close to Him

Scripture: Psalm 51:10; 2 Timothy 2:22; 1 John 3:2-3; Psalm 12:6

Application: What does it mean to be pure? Being pure is being uncontaminated and unpolluted. This means setting ourselves apart from the world to live a life so holy that it glorifies God. Friend, I want to encourage you to let go of the contaminants of this world and get lost in God's love. You see, 1 John 3:2-3 shows us how, if we have such an eagerness and hope in Jesus' return, we will make it our aim to be holy as Jesus is holy. The good news is that we don't have to do it on our own strength. Jesus has given us the Holy Spirit to convict us when we sin or contaminate our spirit. Take David in Psalm 51. He was repenting for the sin he committed with Bathsheba. In this psalm, we learn that even though the man after God's own heart sinned, God was still pleased with Him since He had a repentant heart. Friend, take courage, to become a pure container you only need a willing heart and the Spirit of God in your life. Ask God to show you how you can partner with Him to become a pure container for Him.

50

I've Seen To Much

Jesus,

When I feel like giving up and quitting this race called life, remind me of how you died so that I could make the most of it. Remind me how many times you've met me. And how many times I have felt your presence. Remind me how many times you've answered my prayers. And how many times I've heard your merciful whispers. Remind me how I've seen too much. And heard the Holy Spirit's nudges too many times.

And just like that, you reset my heart. You calibrate it. You adjust it. And suddenly I m all in. I don't hold back -- no matter how hard the future is looking. I decide that I'm all in. I decide that I want to run this race with endurance and perseverance.

For I've felt your presence too many times to stop worshipping just because "I'm not feeling it that day." I've battled too much to give up just because "I haven't seen the promise yet."

So I stand firm in my faith. I do not let circumstances change my hope and crack my foundation. I might not do it perfectly, but I know that you honor and delight in my commitment and trust. So I fix my eyes on you. I do not grow weary and I do not lose heart.

Scripture: Hebrews 12:1-3; John 14:26

Application: Have you had those days when you feel like giving up? Where being a Christian seems harder than not? I encourage you, bring to remembrance all the time God has met you, loved you, and delivered you out of your circumstances. You see, He is for you. He will never let you down. He is running this race *with* you.

51

If The Only Thing I Am Good At

God,

I was asked what was something I was good at. And my first thought was: "Spending time with God." And I know that may not be a popular answer. I know that might not come across as impressive. I know that may not be an accepted answer by the world.

But I've made up my mind, if the only thing I am good at in this world is spending time with you, I am satisfied. If the only accomplishment I have in this world is sitting at your feet and worshipping you, I am content. If the only thing I gained is the knowledge of who you are, I did not lack. If the only thing I am known for is intentionally pursuing you, I did not waste my time.

I pray that you would give me an undivided heart for you alone. I pray that the medications of my heart and the words of my mouth would be pleasing to you. Let me delight in you all the days of my life. Give me the desire to be in your courts. To praise your name. To dance before you. To delight myself in you.

Instill in me a hunger to know the depths of your heart. Engrave the words of your lips in my heart. Remind me that you alone satisfy. You alone is why I live and why I rejoice. For you, my King.

For if the only thing I am good at in this world is spending time with you, I am satisfied.

Scripture: Luke 10:38-42; Psalm 86:11; Psalm 19:14

Application: Meditate on the story of Mary and Martha in Luke 10. Think about how Mary was intentional to spend time with Jesus even when she probably had a million things in her to-do list. You see, we live in an upside-down Kingdom where the things of this world add no value to us, but spending time with Jesus does. He should be our number one priority. He is the only person who can satisfy us. I'm not saying it will be easy, but I encourage you, set time apart for God each day and see what He does with the time you give HIm.

52

I'll Ride The Waves With You

Jesus,

Thank you for your plans for me. Thank you that they are better than what I can expect. Better than what I can dream. Better than what I could ever come up with. Because your thoughts are higher than mine and you see what I can't see.

My plans, You had already ordained them before the foundations of the Earth. You already knew the obstacles I would have to endure and overcome. So I remind myself that nothing that is happening to me right now is a surprise to you. I remind myself that you know the end from the beginning. I remind myself that you have me in the palms of your hand -- as the apple of your eye.

So I decide to ride the wave with you. I don't want to fight it anymore. I don't want to strive to avoid it anymore. I don't want to try to fix it. I don't want to try to let it control me. I decide to just ride it. Messy hair and all. Not knowing all the steps or the direction it's going, but trusting that the one who goes before me will never leave me nor forsake me.

So I decide to ride the wave with you. I choose to trust you. I choose to fix my eyes on you. I choose to let you stretch my faith. I choose to let you guide my path. And I choose to trust that your plans for me are good.

> **Scripture:** Jeremiah 29:11; Isaiah 55:8-9; Hebrews 12:2; Deuteronomy 31:8

> **Application:** How many times have you had plans and it seems like nothing is working out? Your plans get canceled, the relationship fails, your business isn't doing as expected, you are still single. Whatever it is, know that God knows. He sees. But instead of sitting in despair and grief, I encourage you to ride the wave with Him and ask Him to show you what He wants to do in your life in this season. He longs to partner with you! So ask yourself, what disappointment can I choose to let Jesus walk me through instead of sitting on it and letting it take root in your heart?

53

I Love Life With You

Jesus,

Before I knew you, I was not living
The canvas of my life was black and white
My foundation was sinking sand
And my life had no meaning

I questioned every breath I took
Every idle step I walked
I questioned the purpose of my life
Every empty thought in mind

But now that I *know* you, I know what living really is
You painted the canvas of my life with living colors
You gave me a firm foundation in Jesus Christ
And you gave me a hope and a future

So I delight in you, my King
For you make known to me the path of life
You fill me with your fullness of joy
And I rejoice, for your love is better than life itself

I love every breath spent with you
Every step walked with you
Even every cry shed with you
I love life with you

Scripture: Psalm 16

Application: Take a moment to remember your life before Jesus. How did you feel? Where was your hope in? Now, take time to read and meditate on Psalm 16 and give God thanks for being so merciful to call you by name. So merciful to want a relationship with you and give you a new hope and a future. So merciful to give you a delightful inheritance and fill you with joy in His presence. And not just any type of joy, the Hebrew word for joy in Psalm 16:11 is simchah which means exceeding joy, gladness, and mirth, which is gladness accompanied with laughter. You see, He is where the joy is!

54

You Are Sovereign

God,

How sovereign are you Lord, that your plans stand firm forever? How sovereign are you Lord, that you are able to frustrate the plans of the nations? That what you speak comes into existence? That you bring forth life by merely breathing into things? That you speak death and things must wither?

Your plans are always higher than ours Lord. We can plan our lives, but it is your plan that prevails. We can worry about tomorrow, but we are only promised today. We can think that we are in control, but you are the alpha and the omega, the beginning and the end.

We are merely clay waiting to be molded by the master artist. Every crevice and every dent, purposefully created by You. How majestic are your works, my Lord!

We pray for our thoughts to be agreeable with yours. Help us see how you see. Remove our entitlement and prideful mentality. For we are mere humans who wither like the grass and our glory like flowers that fall on the Earth, but you Lord, are sovereign and preeminent.

Scripture: Psalm 33:6-11; Proverbs 16:9; 1 Peter 1:24

Application: We live in a world where entitlement runs rampant. We live our lives making our own plans, trying to climb the success ladder, and become prideful and arrogant. But 2020 was the year the Lord reminded us of His sovereignty and preeminence. You see, our lives are merely a vapor. We are fragile and needy humans who need a Savior, but sometimes we forget that He is in control. We think we can plan our own way and set our own goals until God humbles us. So today, I want to invite you to take time to repent if you have ever felt like you were in control of your life and did not give God all the reigns. Let Him take the wheel of your life and you will not be disappointed.

55

When I Look At You

Jesus,

Thank you for your unchanging love that changes me.

When I look at you my Lord, I can't stay the same. I can't let any bitter roots of envy be rooted in my heart anymore because, You LORD, have promised me a hope and a future — a land filled with milk and honey.

When I fix my eyes on you my Lord, I can't stay the same. I can't hold unforgiveness in my heart anymore, for *you LORD* have forgiven me 1000 times a 1000 — without wavering or second thought.

When I look at you my Lord, I can't stay the same. I can't judge others based on their actions, because you have only offered me unending grace no matter what I've done. The kind that overflows and does not run dry.

When I fix my eyes on you my Lord, I can't stay the same. The appetite for the sins that used to entice me leaves, for I remember how much you suffered to make me white as now — a spotless, holy, and blameless bride.

When I look at you my Lord, I can't stay the same. I can't just live for myself without loving others, for you have offered me a constant friend, Holy Spirit, who loves well. So I can love because You loved me first.

So let me forever look at you, the unchanging one who doesn't let me stay the same.

Scripture: Luke 6:27-38; Hebrews 13:8; 1 John 4:19

Application: Living in this world we are promised hardships and tribulations, but the good news is that God has already overcome the world! How does this apply practically? When we are hurt by the world or our flesh is coming to the surface, we have the opportunity to look at Jesus and with Holy Spirit's help, we are able to forgive, become clean, and have pure hands and hearts. So friend, if you are stuck in a sin pattern or need to forgive, look at Him and let His unchanging love change you!

56

How Could I?

Jesus,

In every season, whether a victory or a failure,
You are more than enough
At the bottom of the valley or the peak of the mountain
You are still the longing of my heart

How could I live without you?
If you stick closer than a brother
You listen without judgment
And you speak with loving wisdom

How could I live without you?
If I earnestly desire your nearness
You are pure living water
The one that always satisfies

I would rather know You alone
Than know the all riches of this world
I would rather give You my heart in its entirety
Than let the things of this world take a hold it

How could I let a day pass without hearing your voice?
How could I let an opportunity go without worshipping you?
You are surely a longing fulfilled
My best friend, my counselor, my prince of peace

Scripture: Proverbs 18:24; Psalm 84:10; Isaiah 9:6

Application: Most of the time when we are going through something or we have a victory we tend to run to a spouse, family, or friends. But friend, God longs to be our top priority. He longs for us to have an undivided heart towards Him and He desires all of our heart. So what does that look like? Going to Him first when you have a victory and thanking Him! Or if you are going through hardship, going to Him first for advice and wisdom. So today ask yourself, am I placing others first before God? If so, what practical steps can I take to place Him first in my life again?

57

How Much Longer?

Jesus,

I try, but I still mess up. I get back up, but I still fall back and keep going to the old. How much more changing do I need? How much longer will it take? Why can't I do, think, and say the right things every time?

And you come closer, wrap your arms around me and say *"Child, it's a journey not a destination. It's a marathon not a sprint. When you get to Heaven you will be holy and perfect as I am. For now, cling to Me and let Me show others how I transform you little by little from the inside out. It's all for My glory in the end. Will you let your life be a living sacrifice for Me?"*

And as a cry before you, you hold me tighter. And as you hold me tighter, your love makes me stronger. For your word says that love covers a multitude of sins. So I know I am loved. I know I am forgiven. I know I am white as snow before you. A spotless bride. For you have removed my sins as far as the east is from the west. So I get back up and run this race with endurance. I cling to you my Jesus, as the anchor of my hope.

Scripture: 2 Timothy 4:7; Hebrews 12:1-3; Psalm 103:12; Hebrews 6:19-20

Application: Have you ever felt as if you fall short? As if you try to live a life pure for God but you keep saying or doing the wrong things? Be encouraged, God promises us that He will change us from the inside out with His spirit, not our own strength. You only have to fix your eyes and cling to Him and He will surely guide you. If this is you today, I encourage you to pray this prayer of repentance, "Father, thank you that you are abounding in love in mercy. I repent for _____ and ask you to wash me clean and give me clean hands and a pure heart. Let my life be a testimony of your transformation power. In Jesus' name. Amen"

58

I Am Set Apart

Jesus,

You chose me before I had the knowledge of how to choose you. Thank you. You made me a chosen people, a holy nation. You set me apart for yourself. You drew me near with an unfailing and everlasting love. Thank you.

You placed a desire in me to worship and love you, unceasingly. Thank you. You have placed a burning in my heart to offer myself as a living sacrifice for you. Thank you.

So I remind myself of the weightiness of this calling. I remind myself that saying no to social gatherings and idle activities are sacrifices that will be worthy in the end. I remind myself that spending endless hours with you at a time is not a waste of time, but rather a privilege and a grace you've placed in me.

So I rejoice in you. I feast on you. I choose to live for you. And I leave the distractions fall off and let you captivate my heart. Over and over again. I let you set my heart apart, for you.

Scripture: Psalm 4:3;1 Peter 2:9; Deuteronomy 14:2; Romans 12:1

Application: If you are reading this, God has chosen you and has set you apart! Rejoice in the fact that God is drawing you near to Him. Even though this is a weighty calling, He does not expect perfection from you. But we should be intentional to be changed as we spend more time with Him, remove lesser lovers, and offer our lives as a living sacrifice. Ask God how you can partner with Him to live a life set apart and pleasing to Him. He is so ready to meet you where you are at!

59

I Want to Please You

Jesus,

I want to please you.

And as soon as I have an open and willing heart, you remind me how pleasing you does not come out of my own striving. You remind me how I don't have to get it right all the time because your grace is sufficient for me. You remind me how I don't have to have unshakeable faith all the time because you are faithful even when I am faithless. You remind me that you are already well pleased with me, even before I do anything for you.

You remind me how pleasing you is a heart posture. Pleasing you is being quick to repent and turn my heart away from sin. Pleasing you is being a woman after your own heart. Pleasing you is offering even the smallest sacrifice of praise amidst my circumstances.

You remind me how pleasing you comes from a willing heart. Pleasing you is taking any effort and opportunity to love you and others well. Pleasing you is having even the smallest mustard seed-sized faith in you. Pleasing you is not getting distracted with affairs that don't concern you, but rather taking the burden of what breaks your heart.

So I give you permission to breathe your love, joy, peace, forbearance, kindness, goodness, faithfulness, gentleness, and self-control into the depths of my heart. So I can please you well, my King.

Scripture: Psalm 51:16-17; Hebrews 13:15-16; 2 Timothy 2:4; Galatians 5:22-23

Application: The Bible clearly shows us how God already died for all our sins and there is nothing we can do for Him to love us more or less. But I do believe we ought to make an effort to please Him -- not from a place of striving but a place of gratitude and love towards Him. So today, ask and allow Him to deposit the fruits of His Spirit in you and declare them over your life.

60

You Multiply

Jesus,

When my heart is gripped by fear of lack, you remind me that what you graciously give you can multiply. You remind me of who you are: Jehovah Jireh, the Lord who provides.

For you Lord, lack is an opportunity for a miracle. It's an opportunity for multiplication. An opportunity for a testimony. For you Lord, lack does not exist.

You remind me how the birds do not bring offerings to you and you still provide for them. You remind me how you supply nutrients for the flowers to flourish and grow without striving. You remind me how the only thing required of me is to seek your kingdom and righteousness, and all things will be given unto me. You remind me of how all you need of me is a little thanksgiving and faith.

So thank you for provision. Thank you for being so intentional in my lack. Thank you for searching around the Earth looking to support and strengthen my heart when I am in need.

Thank you for accepting the little I have as a sacrifice for you. And as I give you my 5 loaves of bread and 2 fishes in thanksgiving, you reach down and breathe on it. You reach down and multiply it.

And you promise me that in the days of famine I will enjoy plenty. You promise me that what I sow I will reap. You multiply what I lack, Jehova Jireh.

Scripture: Matthew 6:25-33; 2 Chronicles 16:9; Psalm 37:19; Matthew 14:13-21

Application: Going through a period of lack is not easy. As humans, it's easier to look at the physical realm instead of using our faith and believing God's word. But today I want to invite you to know the Lord intimately. You see, in Genesis 22, the Lord reveals one of His names to us, Jehova Jieh. This name was given to the Lord by Abraham on Mount Moriah after the Lord provided a substitute for the sacrifice of His son Isaac. You see, right when we think we will end up in lack, our God is one to surprise us and provide exactly what we need. So what do we do in the meantime? We see in Matthew 6 how Jesus, in the midst of lack, decided to place His eyes above, give thanks and have faith. So friend, I want to invite you to do the same today and see how the LORD provides.

61

Nothing is Wasted

Jesus,

With you, nothing is wasted.

Every time I decided to spend time with You instead of watching a movie, You acknowledged it. Nothing was wasted.

Every time I skipped a social event to spend my weekends worshipping you, you acknowledged it. Nothing was wasted.

Every time I dropped everything at hand — responsibilities, chores, cares — to commune with you, You acknowledge it. Nothing was wasted.

Every time I tithed instead of using that money to pay bills, You acknowledged it. Nothing was wasted.

Thank you that even if I was misunderstood by others, I gained everything. Thank you that even if I abided by your commands but did not fit in, I gained everything. Thank you that even if I spent all my free time with you and did not fit in with the culture, I gained everything. Because with you Lord, nothing is wasted.

I pray that my heart would continue to be drawn to you, that my spirit would continue to long for you, and that I would continue wasting my perfume on you, Jesus. Because with you, nothing is wasted.

Scripture: Matthew 19:29; John 12:3-8; 1 Corinthians 15:58

Application: Friend, how are you wasting yourself and your time on Jesus today? We have to realize that Jesus delights in spending time with us. He delights when we choose Him over the temporary pleasures of this word. You see, He saw every time you chose Him over events, people, and entertainment. This does not mean you don't enjoy friendships or social events, but it does mean we have to say no to some things to say yes to Him! So ask Jesus to show and reveal to you anything that is hindering this communion and/or how you can be more intentional to spend time with Him.

62

Speak

Jesus

I wake up with an expectant heart
For I know you will speak
I go about my day expecting to hear your voice
For it's like sweet melodies to my ears

I lay down at night thinking of you
For I know you are near and desire to speak
I ask you for dreams and visions
To be part of your inner circle

So speak Lord
For I am listening
Whisper your secrets in my ear
For I long to steward them

Your words Lord are what keeps the fire in my soul
The motivation to take every step
What keeps me going every day
For your voice Jesus is what sustains my soul

So speak Lord
For I am listening
Invade my thoughts by day
And my dreams by night

Speak Lord
I am listening

Scripture: John 10:27; Psalm 5:3; Jeremiah 33:3

Application: Are you attuned and tethered to God's voice? Do you wake up and go to bed expecting to hear Him through whispers, other people, dreams, visions? Friend, if you have not experienced His voice or want to experience it in a deeper way, ask Him! Say "Father, I am submitting my mind and my ears to you. Remove any mindsets that are blocking me from perceiving and listening to your heart towards me. I declare I hear your voice in a new and fresh way. Amen." Now, thank God for this new gift or for the increase of it!

63

My Calling

God,

You intricately made me in my mother's womb. You instilled in me a purpose and a future. You gave me gifts and talents. Desires and passions. Hopes and dreams. You planned good works for me to walk into.

So do not let me grow cold towards them. Do not let me grow numb to them. Don't let me forget why you created me. No matter how hard or impossible it seems to accomplish them. Remind me that if you called me to it, you will fulfill them through me.

My prayer is that if I ever choose to forget those dreams and passions, that you would ignite a fire in me. That you would make my heart beat again for those plans. That you would instill such a zeal to please you in fulfilling them with you.

Remind me how you have placed a unique spirit in me that only I carry. A spirit full of love and encouragement for people. Full of the desire to serve you and please you.

So I let go of paradigms and negative mindsets that tell me I am not good enough. Those that tell me that my calling and giftings do not matter. And I declare I will fulfill the calling you have placed in me through your Holy Spirit.

Scripture: Psalm 139:13-16; Ephesians 2:10; Psalm 138:8 (ESV)

Application: Sometimes we let this world discourage and distract us from the plans God has placed in our hearts. Other times we think to ourselves "Why bother with this when so many other people are doing it?" But the truth is, God has placed specific people in your path that only you can bless. There is something only you have that can change someone else's life. So today, write down those desires, hopes, dreams, and that calling God has placed in your heart and ask Him to reveal to you how to get there —what first steps can you be intentional with this week?

64

I Want it Your Way

Jesus,

I give up. I'm done trying to make it work my way only to get disappointed. I'm done forcing things that you don't want for me. I'm done trying to accelerate your timing.

So I let go of my expectations of how things should happen. I let go of my reasoning of how you will work. I let go of all entitlement of why I should have certain things. And I humble myself towards you.

I'm done striving.
I want it your way.

Thank you, Lord, that as I surrender, you quiet my soul. And I become like a weaned child who no longer cries for its mother's milk. I become content. Satisfied.

You come in and offer me a resting place. You make me lie down in green pastures and refresh my soul. You accept me as I am and where I am at. You open your arms and let me lean on your chest, My Good Shepherd.

And as soon as I surrender, you work on my behalf. You do more than I could ever imagine. And you surprise me. You blow my expectations. That's just who you are -- the One who goes above and beyond.

Scripture: Psalm 23 TPT; Psalm 131; Ephesians 3:20

Applications: I wrote this when I was letting the details and timing of things get ahold of my peace. I let fear and control take the place of my trust in Jesus. So friend, if you can relate ask yourself, why I am striving? Do we not trust God enough? You see, I had to ask myself those hard questions. The good news is that God loves us even when we are faithless. And today He is inviting you to let go of expectations He might not have given you. Let go of control. And lean on His chest while you meditate on Psalm 23 (TPT).

65

What Kind of God Are You?

Jesus,

Thank you for humbling yourself to remove the veil that separated us. Thank you for fighting the darkness of legalism and sin to have a relationship with us. But what is human life but a mist that vanishes?

What kind of God are you that you concern yourself with us, unfaithful lovers? What kind of God are you that you would occupy your thoughts on us? What kind of God are you that you would collect our tears in a bottle? For our human life is like a temporary mist that vanishes at your appointed time.

What kind of God would step down from Heaven to commune with us, mere dust? What kind of God would willingly inhabit in our sinful bodies and wicked hearts?

Jesus, help us see the magnitude of your sacrifice. Help us see how we can't even be faithful without your help. Help us see how we are nothing without you. Help us realize that we can only love you because you loved us first.

Scripture: Matthew 27:51, Psalm 139:17; Psalm 8:4; James 4:14

Application: Have you pondered on the fact that the God of the universe does not give up on you? Regardless of our wicked, sinful heart, He decided to reside on you and I. He keeps taking care of you and me. He keeps thinking about us. He keeps comforting us. Regardless of how little we can offer. Or I should say, regardless of the fact that we can't offer anything worthy of Him. Take time to thank and praise Him for this relationship.

66

Make It Look Like You

Jesus,

Wrap my whole world in your arms
And make it look like you
So when people see it
They see a reflection of who you are

Place your thoughts in my mind
And make me think like you
So that when people hear me speak
They hear your spirit speaking to their heart

Put your finger in every area of my life
And make it look like you
So that every eye would see
And every tongue would confess your name

Let me be the essence of who you are
Let me humbly bring glory to your name
Let me be who you've called me to be
Let me be one of the few who shares the good news

Make my life look like you

Scripture: 2 Corinthians 3:18; Psalm 19:14; Philippians 2:10-11

Applications: Sometimes as Christians we think of sharing the gospel as a scary, intimidating, and complicated thing. When in reality, when we follow Jesus and are intentional about looking more like Him from a place of rest, trust, and faith, we allow other people to see a glimpse of Him through us! How many of us have been asked "what's different about you?" or told, "I want what you have." That's the Jesus in us! So don't overcomplicate sharing the gospel. Go and be the hands and feet of Jesus to others and let God, through you, do the work.

67

In the Little

Jesus,

Help me see you in the little
Even in what seems insignificant
Help me see you in the lack
Even when it seems like I don't have enough

Let me be a good and faithful servant
Don't let me forsake the times of small beginnings
Those special moments where it's you and I
Those small victories won by your side

Let me steward your heart well
Don't let me take your presence for granted
Even when it's only you and I
I want you to be right by my side

Let me steward the talents you have given me
I want to use them well — multiply them for you
I want to make you proud
So let me honor you well in the little

Scripture: Matthew 25:14-30; Luke 16:10

Application: The Bible tells us how if we are faithful with the little, God will give us much more. Even in the parable of the talents, Jesus is pleased when His servants multiply what He has given them. So friend, how is your attitude in the little? Are you frustrated? Ungrateful? How are you stewarding God's presence now if you want more of it in the future? How are you taking care of the circle of influence He has given you if you want to pour into more further down the road? I challenge you, be thankful and intentional about what He has given you now so He can give you more of Himself and His Kingdom. Let's be good and faithful servants.

68

I Don't Want To

Jesus,

I don't want to feel like I have it all together
I don't want to feel like I know what's best
I don't want to feel like I don't need you
Remind me that only with you I am blessed

Come in and remove all my pride
Bring me down to my knees
Remove my self-righteousness
And make me lean on you instead of me

I don't want to trust in horses & chariots
I don't want to place my trust in this world
I don't want to rely on my own strength
Remind me to trust in you alone

Come in and expose my deceitful heart
Make me realize I am nothing without you
Allow me to fail once in a while
Remind me that you show favor to the humble

So I choose to not lean on my own understanding
I choose to live not by what I see but by what you say

I choose to trust you even when it does not make sense
I choose faith over sight, your whispers over human wisdom

Thank you for not allowing me to be wise in my own eyes
Thank you for reminding me that your foolishness is wiser than
human wisdom

Scripture: Psalm 20:7; Proverbs 3:5-6; 2 Corinthians 5:7;
Proverbs 3:7; 1 Corinthians 1:25

Application: How many times do we think we know better
than God? We become fearful of trusting HIm since what
we see in the natural world does not align with what He is
saying. We think, "God that would not work" or "God that
does not make sense." But friend, let me remind you that
even the foolishness of God is wiser than human wisdom.
Just as he gave the Israelites Jericho by marching 7 times,
told Noah to build an arc, and used a Samaritan woman to
spread His teachings so He can use the world's foolishness
to bring out your breakthrough. So I encourage you, humble
yourself before Almighty God, submit your plans to Him,
and don't lean on your own understanding. What He is
asking of you might not make sense, but it will surely work
out for your good. That is His nature.

69

If You Send Me, I'll Go

God,

All around the world,
Men and woman living for themselves
Not knowing the joy of walking with you
Nor the honor of living for you

Build a hunger in these people for you alone
Reveal yourself to them
Let them see visions and dreams
Let them sense your tangible presence

Show up God so that none will perish
Open their eyes and remove the veil
Let them see you clearly
So that they can praise your name

If you send me Father, I'll go
Prepare the soil of hearts, soften up walls
Let me plant seeds of your love
Let me see them flourish for you

Only you can spring life in unfertile ground
So give me your heart for the nations Jesus
Stir my heart for what moves yours
If you send me I'll go

Scripture: Psalm 67; 2 Peter 3:9

Application: As believers, we were commanded by Jesus to go out, share the good news, and make disciples. But I wonder, how many of us are actually doing this? Are we being faithful servants of Jesus or are we just being comfortable? Friend, I encourage you to get out of your comfort zone and share the good news. If you have a passion for the nations coming to know Jesus, ask Him to send you. If you don't, ask Him to give you the desires of His heart and consider sowing in other ways such as financial offerings to those who are willing. Everyone has a part to play to see the nations come to know Him. Today, ask Him to reveal your part.

70

Let Israel Know You

God,

Thank you for your nation of Israel, your chosen people. Those who you've set apart and guarded since the beginning of time. Those you've suffered and grieved with during times of tribulation, suffering, and persecution over all these years. Those you've cried out for a relationship with your son Jesus, waiting for them to see who He really is, their messiah and their Savior. We bless them today.

Most of all, thank you for choosing us, mere gentiles, to go before them and provoke them to jealousy. Father, give us the faith and boldness to go and share your good news. Let us not just "bless" Israel by sending money, but rather by financially supporting missionaries or becoming one ourselves! Let us see how this is our calling in life, to share the good news.

We ask that you would start showing up in their lives. Give them dreams, visions, and let them hear your voice. May they come to know you. May the prophecies be fulfilled. May the remnant, your bride, gather again in Israel in time for the coming of the bridegroom. Let them be ready.

And thank you for being slow to fulfill your promises so that no one shall perish.

Scripture: Romans 10-11

Application: As we know, Israel is God's holy nation and chosen people but unfortunately most of them do not know Jesus and therefore are not saved. Statistically, only about 0.3% of Jews are messianic Jews. So what is our role here? Friend, I want to encourage you to pray not only for Israel but for the Arabs, from the bloodline of Ishmael, who have fought against them for so many years. Not only this but if we can, let's make it our goal to go to Israel and share the good news. If this is not feasible for you, let's support missionaries who are evangelizing in Israel or in other Jew-prominent areas (Romans 10:14-15). And friend, if you do not have a heart or yearning for Israel to come to know Jesus, I pray that God would place that longing in you and make your heartburn for what burns His.

71

You Are My Healer

God,

Thank you for your healing power and the authority you have given me to cast out sickness. I acknowledge that sickness does not come from you, but rather, it has to bow down to your name. It has to tremble at your feet. It has to leave.

Thank you Jesus for defeating disease 2021 years ago. Every stripe on your back represents every illness you have conquered. Every shed drop of blood reminds me of how your blood speaks a better word. So I remind myself, by your wounds I am healed.

I thank you for healing. Thank you for restoring me from my bed of illness. Thank you for coming in close. Even when the world thinks it's impossible and when I don't feel like you can come through. You still come through. You still heal. For it's in your nature, Jehovah Rapha. My Great Physician.

> **Scripture:** Matthew 10:1; Psalm 103:1-4; Isaiah 53:5; Exodus 15:26

Application: If you need a miracle today, I am standing with you. God is near and ready to heal. He said in His word how He has given us authority to cast out illness. So friend, ask God right now to come close and demand any illness to come out of you. It has no authority over your life or your body. The Spirit of the Almighty God is inside of you so anything that is not from Him leaves in Jesus name. Remember, He is Jehovah Rapha, the Lord Who Heals.

72

In the Disappointment

God,

Thank you for the disappointments. Those times when I did not get what I thought was for me. Those times I was hurt by someone I loved. Those times my expectations did not match my reality.

Thank you for those times, because in the midst of them, you were so close. So near. Ready to love. Ready to heal. It was in those times that I saw you as a comforter and a loving Father.

And in those times You always remind me that I have a choice. A choice to trust you in the midst of disappointment or to harbor bitterness in my heart and make my heart sick. I always have a choice. So I chose you. I chose the option that involves you.

So I strip off all the times my heart was filled with hope deferred and lay them at your feet. And as I do, You remind me how You are the anchor of my soul. You are a shield around me and the lifter of my head. You are the one that goes before me and arranges a table in the presence of my enemies.

So I choose you. Time and time again. I choose you in the hurt. I choose you in the betrayal. I choose you in disappointment.

Scripture: Hebrews 6:19; Psalm 3:13; Psalm 23:5; Proverbs 13:12

Application: I wrote this during a season when someone else got what I thought was mine. Yes, it was hard and painful, but it made me stronger. I learned that I had a choice. A choice to harbor resentment in my heart or a choice to bless that person and trust God. Friend, you always have a choice. So encourage you, just like David was not invited to his own party and kept being faithful to God. You continue walking out your life with Jesus as the anchor for your soul, because friend, He will never disappoint you. Instead, He will make your cup overflow.

73

Pregnant with Purpose

God,

Thank you for purpose
And thank you for impregnating me with it

There's such a calling you have instilled in me
And it's not small
There's such zeal for purpose in my Spirit
Don't let me lose heart

Search within the deepest parts of my soul
Change me
Refine me
Build me up

Help me partner with you
Help me speak it into existence

I want to please you
I want to fulfill what you have placed in me
Every thought, desire, and every word
Let me be one of the few who fulfills it

Don't let me give up on it
Don't let my life go to waste

I feel you working in me
I feel you refining me
In the waiting
In the equipping

Because you have called me
You will bring it to pass
Because you have placed it in my heart
You will fulfill it

Scripture: Jeremiah 29:11; Ecclesiastes 3:11; Psalm 138:8 (ESV)

Application: I wrote this in a season where I felt pregnant with purpose. I knew I had a lot to give and that God was working in me to produce fruit but was not sure what the fruit would look like. Have you ever been in that situation? Maybe you are asking God how He wants you to serve or what is your next career move or what profession to study. Friend, let me encourage you and remind you that what He began in you He will complete. He is not a man that he should lie. Scripture tells us that He has placed eternity in your heart and planned your good deeds even before you were born. So today, partner with Him, stand in faith, and declare the promises He has spoken over you. Even if you have not seen the fruit, know that He is watering your seed.

74

I Don't Want to Fall Out of Love

Jesus,

I don't want to fall out of love with you
I don't want to grow numb to your presence
Don't let me forsake You
Or be indifferent to your very essence

Remind me of those times
When it was only you and I
Those days when only you mattered
And when you were my only living water

Let me feel you as in the beginning
When the butterflies of this first love were so present
Remind me of all the reasons why I fell in love with you
And woe me back into your presence

Instill in me a desire to dwell in your courts forever
To gaze upon and rejoice in your beauty
For you have never left a desire unmet
You have been able to satisfy them all

So I keep coming before You
Day in and day out
No matter how I feel, I only ask one thing
I don't want to fall out of love with your presence

Scripture: Psalm 27:4; Psalm 63:1

Application: I wrote this prayer when I was feeling numb to God's presence. My heart felt hardened. No song would soften it. No prayer made a difference in my sight, but I knew I still needed to sit at his feet. So I did. And this came out. Friend, I want to remind you how we need God's help to even be able to love God. Know that even when you don't feel Him, He is still there, right next to you. Today, repent if you have placed lesser lovers before Him and pray to fall more in love with Him today. I want to encourage you, be intentional to pursue Him and He will surely come and pursue you back!

75

You Are The God That Sees Me

Jesus,

When I feel forgotten
When I feel like I don't matter
When I feel like I am not favored
When I feel like I am not making a difference

Remind me that you are El Roi
The God who *sees* me
The God who looks for me
And the God who is intentional to meet me

Remind me that your eyes have not moved from me,
But rather my eyes have wandered from you
Remind me that your gaze has remained constant on me,
But my focus has shifted from you

So I thank you Lord
For always aligning my heart with yours
For removing the fog from my eyes & giving me your perspective
And for reminding me that the only eyes I need on me, are yours

So when I feel unseen I remind myself that you are El Roi, the
God who *sees* me

Scripture: Genesis 16 (emphasize v 13-14)

Application: Read the story of Hagar and Sarah and ask yourself, have you ever felt unseen, unloved, and forgotten? You see, that's how Hagar felt after Sarah mistreated her, but that was not the case. God had always had her eyes on her. God saw her, loved her, and pursued her. You see when we feel forgotten it's because we have shifted our gaze from God to our circumstances. So I encourage you, today, shift your focus back to Him and let Him remind you that His eyes have always been right on you.

76

You Satisfy

Jesus,

Every time I enter your courts, I come in hungry but go out satisfied. You speak to my soul. You make it align to your Spirit. You fill me with yourself and I am once again content.

Every time I enter your courts, I come in weak but go out strong. You infuse strength into my bones. You remind me that when I am weak, you are strong. That when I surrender, you thrive in my circumstances.

Every time I enter your courts, I come in confused but leave with a sound mind. You remind me that when I acknowledge you in all my ways, you make my path straight. That when I don't know where I am going, you have already made a way for me. That you walk before, behind, and even alongside me.

And when I feel myself growing distant from you — finding fulfillment in the fleeting things of this world — you are merciful to lure me back to your throne. Like a compass, you pull me back to where I am supposed to be — your presence. Not in a condescending way, but with a gentle Spirit. You tug on the strings of my heart and whisper in my soul. And I am undone. I run back to you. I remember your goodness, what you've done, and how you've loved.

Thank you — for never leaving my side, for never leaving a desire unmet, for never walking away, but rather pressing in.

Scripture: Psalm 23; 2 Corinthians 12:9-11; Proverbs 3:6, Psalm 63

Application: When Jesus died and was resurrected, He opened the door for a blameless and righteous relationship with the Father. Not only that, but He left His Holy Spirit to live in us and reminded us of His body and blood as a symbol of Himself. You see, when we feel empty and unsatisfied, it's because we are not feeding our Spirit, we are letting the things of this world try to fill us. Friend, I invite you to partake of His meal and remember the sacrifice He did for you. Out of this, you will be satisfied as with the riches of meals.

77

I Surrender: Not My Will

God,

Thank you for giving me free will, but I don't want it. I want your will in my life. So I surrender to you: my life, my desires, my wants, my plans, my timeline. I surrender it all.

I just want you. I want what you want. I want what you predestined for me. I want what you appointed for me. For I know that you know best. I know that you know what my heart needs. So I choose to let go of my expectations of how things should go and how things should unfold.

I'm done choosing the foolish things of this world and let you choose for me. I trust you, the One who made me. The One who created me and took pleasure in my birth. The One who made me with a purpose and a plan. The One who appointed me and made me for such a time like this.

I trust you. For not one of your promises have ever failed. Not one of your plans has ever been thwarted. You always finish what you start. You always take pride in your creation. You are intentional with your children. And you will not put me to shame, for my hope is in you alone.

Scripture: Psalm 131; Romans 10:11; Matthew 10:39

Application: Psalm 131 is one of my favorite scriptures. Why? Well, it shows us how David chose to surrender his will to God. He chose not to concern himself with things that were too complicated or lofty for Him and merely surrendered to God. He basically quieted his soul, which are His desires, plans, and ambitions that maybe were not happening at that time. So instead of fighting against God's timing and his ways, He chose to surrender. Friend, I encourage you, surrender your will to God. The word says that we gain our life when we lose it. So take heart, trust in the Lord, and let Him write your story.

78

How Can I Wash Your Feet?

Jesus,

You have done so much for me
You have loved me unconditionally
You accepted me when everyone rejected me
You called me by name and made me righteous

What can I do for you?
How can I repay you?

And I hear you say:
I just want your heart
I just want your time
I just want your yes

So I bow down and declare:
I will waste my life on you Lord
I will spill my perfume on your feet
I will whisper love letters in your ears

How can I be a living sacrifice?
How can I live for you alone?

And I hear you say:
A daily yes is all I ask
A willing and humble heart is all it takes
A giving spirit without expecting anything back

So I lay it all down for you
My time, my yes, my heart
And I decide to live a life for you
With clean hands and a pure heart

Scripture: John 12:1-11

Application: In John 12 we read the story of Mary anointing Jesus' feet with perfume. You see, Mary had a revelation of the significance of worshipping Jesus. She used what was costly to her and "wasted it" at Jesus' feet. How come? Because she knew Jesus was more significant. He would die for her, redeem her, forgive her of all her sins and make her righteous in front of the Father. That, my friend, is more costly than your most expensive possession. More costly than your time, sleep, and wants. Friend, I encourage you, ask Jesus how you can wash His feet and decide to waste your time, heart, emotions, resources and breath on Him. He is worthy.

79

Fully Persuaded

God,

When I start to doubt your plans for my life
I remind myself of the truth
You are not a man that you should lie
Or a human being to change your mind

You know the end from the beginning
Yet you still care about the middle
You came up with the whole puzzle
Yet you are intentional with every piece

You have already written my story
And you have already been glorified in it
Even when the pieces seem messy
You turn it all for my good

I choose to trust your goodness
I do not look at my circumstances
I don't base your plans for me on my emotions
My sight does not get to scream louder than your words

But instead, I become fully persuaded
That your plans for me are good

For you have promised
And you can't go against your nature

Thank you for following through
Even to the slightest detail
Promise keeper
Faithful one

Scripture: Numbers 23:19; Romans 4:18-22; Genesis 15:6-21

Application: I wrote this one of those days when I needed to build my faith up and remind my soul to align to what God says. One of those days when I had to stop living by what I saw and become fully persuaded of what God had promised. You see, in Romans 4, we are reminded of how Abraham, even though his body was weak, did not waver in unbelief regarding God's promise. Why? Because God had made him a promise unto Himself. In Genesis 15 we see how God made a covenant with Abraham and instead of making Abraham go through the pieces of the cut animals (typically the servant did this part, not God), only God did. What was He saying? Basically, that He, God, was swearing on Himself that if He or Abraham did not do part of the covenant, He would assume the responsibility. Isn't that mind-blowing! God wanted to let Abraham know how serious and real He was about the promise. So today, rest in His faithfulness and sovereignty over your promise.

80

You Fill Me Up

Holy Spirit,

You fill me up
Not wealth or status
Not a husband or friend
Not followers or likes

I've realized nothing in this world can satisfy me like you
Your whispers in my ear when I feel unseen
Your presence when I can't feel anything
Your living water when I feel dry and unclean

I wouldn't trade it for anything
Not riches
Not success
Not social status

I've tasted and I've seen
I've had a drink from the One true source
The only One that has living water
The only One that quenches my thirst

You fill me up
To overflow

I don't have to thirst again
For you are the flow that never ends

Scripture: John 4:14

Application: Have you ever felt empty? Unsatisfied with the things the world offers? Friend, let me remind you that living for this world will never satisfy the deep longing in your heart. As soon as we take our eyes off of the One true source — the living water — we start basing our worth and value on insignificant and trivial things. You see, when you focus and spend time with the living source you don't look around for lesser lovers, since you have found the real thing. Friend, I encourage you to ponder and pray John 4:14 over yourself and ask the LORD what does "drinking His water" looks like in this season of your life.

81

I Want To Be Known

Jesus,

I want to be known as the one who chose you
Even when it was popular not to
I want to be known as the one who never rejected you
Even when everyone around me turned away from you

I want to be known as the one who always told you yes
Regardless of my to-do list and stress
I want to be known for laying down my life for you
Regardless of whether or not you came through

I want to be known as the one who yielded to your presence
The one who never forsook your very essence
I want to be known as the one who chose you as the better thing
By always running and staying at your feet

Let me never forsake the secret place
But rather, help me always crave gazing upon your face
Let me never stop getting on my knees
For I want to always be undone by your heart towards me

I want to be known as the one who loved you well
So help me choose your presence, to dwell

Scripture: Matthew 9:9

Application: Read the story of the calling of Matthew by Jesus. Isn't it wind blowing and convicting how Matthew, a sinner and tax collector, dropped everything to serve Jesus even when it was the least popular thing to do? You see, Matthew was well off financially, was working under the Roman government, and had authority over Jews in his workplace. Regardless of what the world could offer, his tasks, and his obligations, he chose the better thing. He chose to follow Jesus regardless of what everyone thought about his decision. Today, ask yourself, am I known for dropping everything for Jesus? If not, what is holding me back from following Jesus fully? Ask the Holy Spirit to reveal those areas in your heart.

82

There's No Plan B

Jesus,

Other than You alone
There is no plan B for me
Other than You alone
There is no second option for me

So I place all my eggs in your basket
With full confidence in Your nature
You've never let me down
And you won't start now

And even though other options come my way
I continue to place all my hopes & dreams on you
I don't doubt your ability to come through
And I don't waver in unbelief regarding what you say

For You are not a man that you should lie
Nor have You changed your mind
You are a covenant-keeping God
Who follows through every time

Scripture: Number 23:19; Deuteronomy 7:9; Joshua 21:45

Application: Have you ever felt like you were unsure if God was going to fulfill His promises to you? Have you ever felt tempted to do things on your own strength or find another route? Friend, don't make the same mistake as Sarah in Genesis 16. Instead of waiting on God to give her an Isaac, she got creative and told Abraham to have sex with her servant Hagar. You see, it might seem like a small disobedience, but out Ishmael came the Arabs, most of the Muslims, and the cause of most of the war I the Middle East. So if you had moved your eggs to other baskets, He is inviting you today to remember His words, come back to Him, and make Him your Plan A — the only plan.

83

You Have My Permission

Jesus,

Don't let me move again
From your presence, where I belong
Hold me tight
You have my permission

Pursue me and woe me
Just like the old times
Where I would run to your feet
And be completely satisfied

Help me be tethered to your heart
Make your presence addicting to me
Make me burn for you
And you alone my King

For you are good at filling me up
And never leaving me dry
You even make me overflow
You truly satisfy

Don't let me move again
From your presence, where I belong

Hold me tight
You have my permission

Scripture: Exodus 33:12-16; Psalm 27:4

Application: Have you ever felt like you were drifting from Jesus? Not in a drastic way, but to the point of not giving Him priority with your time? You feel hungry spiritually and the things of the world do not fill you up. Life keeps getting busier, and you keep getting emptier. Friend, I've been there. The good news is that Jesus is always close. He has not moved, but sometimes we do. I encourage you to fight the good fight to stay close to Jesus. Make a commitment to pursue Him as He pursues you. Let's be like Moses who did not want to move if God did not go with him. And let's be like David who knew that being in God's presence was the most satisfying experience in this life.

84

You Are Praying For Me

Jesus,

When I am in the middle of a storm
I remind myself of truth
Just as you prayed for Peter
You are praying for me too

You don't leave me stranded
You are with me day and night
You pray for me constantly
So that my faith won't run dry

You don't leave me weak
You don't leave me hurting
You breathe life into my Spirit
So that my life can display your glory

It wasn't enough to humble yourself and die for me
For you even pray for me
As you waste your breath on me
I pray I can waste my life on you

Scripture: Luke 22:31-32

Application: Have you ever thought about the fact that Jesus *prays* for you? Do we even deserve that? In Luke 22 we see how Jesus has already prayed for Peter once He knows the enemy has asked to "sift" Peter. Even now, Jesus humbles himself, even more, to pray for us — sinful humans — just so we can overcome trials. Friend, whatever you are going through today, know that Jesus already knew it was coming and has prayed for you so that your faith might not fail.

85

You Pursued Me

Jesus,

You chose me before I was formed
Even knowing my future transgressions
You loved me before I knew I was lovable
Even in the midst of my failures

And out of so many choices
You chose to call *me* close
In the midst of my indifference
You *still* ran after me

I'm in awe of your pursuit of me
You kept knocking on the door of my heart
Never growing tired of weary
But patiently waiting for my response

You were a gentleman
Never barging in uninvited
But rather waiting with anticipation
For the day when I would let you in

And one day I realized I was empty

Nothing in this world would satisfied
So in the quiet, I heard you whisper my name
And I decided to give you all of my heart

So thank you for pursuing me
Thank you for choosing me
Thank you for loving me
My King

Scripture: Ephesians 1:3-4; Matthew 22:14; John 6:44

Application: Have you ever thought of how intentional God was in pursuing a relationship with you? Sometimes we don't give much thought to it and think it was our doing — we went to church or someone introduced Him to us. But the reality is that He has chosen you and called your name multiple times before you paid attention and accepted the invitation. And in the process, He did not get tired of chasing after you. Meditate on the scriptures for today, thank God for how He met you and invited you in, and commit to pursue Him every day.

86

You Call Me Higher

Jesus,

My hope and my trust are all in you
You never leave nor disappoint

When I rely on myself & fall down
You are faithful to pick me back up

You don't harbor resentment
You are not ashamed of me

You don't accuse
You don't judge

Instead, you call me by name
And you call me higher

You call me closer
And you call me daughter

You see me pure
And you call me righteous

You love me where I am
But also call me higher

Forgive me for doing things my own way
Instead of leaning on you

Help me trust you well
And in your presence always dwell

Scripture: Prov 28:26; Romans 8:1

Application: How many of us have tried to do things on our own strength to only end up failing or worse than before? How many of us have rushed to do things without asking the Lord? Friend, I've been there. But I've learned that the Lord is still gracious. He is loving. He does not condemn us but rather brings us closer to him. So whatever it is that you are going through — no matter if it is your fault or not — know that God sees you, is full of mercy, and is calling you closer. Go lean on Him and let Him wipe your tears away. Let Him call you higher.

87

I Want All

Jesus,

I want *all* the mysteries you have for me. All the words. All the whispers. All the wisdom. I want *all* the affections you have for me. All your touches. All your "I love yous." "All your "I am so proud of yous."

I don't wanna do life on my own. It's not the same. It's not worth it. Listening to your voice is what makes life worth living. Feeling your presence is what makes life bearable. Feeling your comfort is what makes life sweeter.

I want *all* the opportunities you have laid out for me. To encourage people. To speak life into them. To love them well. I want *all* the works you have prepared for me. All the assignments that have my name written on them. Don't let me miss them.

I don't want to live life for my own comfort. It's not the same. It's not worth it. Doing what you have called me to do is food to my body. Being obedient to my calling is what my soul longs for.

Scripture: Romans 5:8-10; Ephesians 2:10; John 4:34; Psalm 27:4

Application: Even though we were sinners, Christ died for us so we could be in relationship with Him (Romans 5:8-10). And that was not enough for Him. He also invited us to bring Heaven on Earth, bring the gospel to nations, and fulfill the works He planned for us in advance to fulfill (Ephesians 2:10). How humbling is that? But sometimes we walk through life trying to fulfill our own desires and ambitions instead of realizing that all our soul and spirit desire is all He has for us — a relationship with Almighty God and to do His good works. Even Jesus said, my food is to do the will of the Father (John 4:34). So friend, draw close to Him and ask Him to reveal those mysteries He has instore for you. And once you've had a revelation of His call for your life and His love for you, act on it!

88

My Oasis

Jesus,

In the middle of the desert
When I had started living for myself
I find you waiting with open arms
My oasis

No judgment in your eyes
No condemnation in your tone
But a heart full of pure love
Eyes full of mercy

For you have felt every emotion I have felt
Every time I have wept, you wept with me
Every time I felt confused, you prayed for me
Every time I sinned against you, you forgave me

In the middle of the desert I find you, my oasis
The only one who can satisfy me
The only one who can love me in my sin
The only one who can forgive my iniquities

Jesus, Nothing can satisfy as much as you can
No one can love as well as you do

No one can leave me as full as you do
In your presence, I find my oasis

Even when I'm not trusting you, you still want me
You still want my breath calling out your name
Even when I'm not placing you first, You still want me
Not only my company but my heart

So I surrender once again, my oasis

Scripture: John 4:14

Application: Have you ever wondered from God? Moved from His presence? Have you ever felt like living for Him, waiting on His promises, and fighting the good fight of faith was too hard? I know I have. The good news is that every time we move away from God, He draws in closer. You see, He is not mad at us. He knows we are mere dust and our sinful nature. But the good news is that His nature is love. He forgives. And He restores. You see, John 4:14 reminds us of how He is the only source of living water who satisfies — our oasis. There is no other thing, person, event that could do that for us. So today, ask God to forgive you of any sins that have made you move you away from Him and realize that He *has not* moved from you.

89

I Live For Your Attention

God,

I am done seeking the admiration of people
I want to live to get a hold of *your* attention
I want to live to catch your gaze
I want to live to make you smile

So I will dance a dance for you
So I will pray a little prayer to you
So I will sing a song for you
Father, Are you looking yet?

I want to live to draw you near
So I will worship you in your house
I want to live to make you proud
So I will live to encourage others

I want to live to love you well
So I will waste my time on you
I want to live to make you make a difference
So I will share your good news

I want to live to get ahold of your attention
And in the midst of all my doing

I hear you say
Daughter, I've never moved my eyes from you

Scripture: 2 Chronicles 16:9

Application: I wrote this in a season when I was spending a significant amount of time with God, but wondering if He was even watching? Because sometimes it felt like He was not. Friend, if you feel the same, I want to remind you that God's eyes have never wandered from you. He has always been near. The Bible tells us how God the "eyes of the LORD search the whole earth in order to strengthen those whose hearts are fully committed to him." So when you feel like He is not watching, just look up and lock eyes with Him.

90

Lovesick

Jesus,

Thank you for loving me. Thank you for always coming. Thank you for being such a faithful lover. A faithful friend. A faithful bridegroom.

I am so lovesick. I am so in love. I am so dependent on you alone. I wake up and can't wait to hear from you. I go about my day and can't stop thinking about you. I go to bed and ask you for dreams. I can't wait to be with you, fully present.

I daydream of the day when I get to spend all the minutes of my day gazing on your beauty. The day when I get to join the heavenly angels singing you praises. The day when I have the privilege of communing with you face to face, no distractions. No second motives. Just pure love. Pure worship.

You quench my deepest longings. My deepest desires. You accept me fully for who I am yet you call me higher. You don't expect me to be someone I am not. Rather, you call me by name and by who you made me to be. You long to hear my voice even when I don't get things right. You desire to have communion even when I am distant and am not intentional with you.

I am so lovesick. I am so in love. I am so dependent on you alone.

Scripture: Psalm 84 (TPT)

Application: After reading Psalm 84, ask yourself: Have you found the one your heart beats for? The one who created you and loves you? The only one who can satisfy you? You see, when you let Jesus pursue you, you can't help but end up lovesick. You can't help but want to be with him constantly -- sharing every breath, every moment, every second. I encourage you, make room for God to pursue your heart today.

91

Letting Go

*If you have ever let go of a relationship, this is for you.

Friend,

Bittersweet. The day you decide to move on from what has seemed an eternity. It's been your normal for so long. You can feel it leave the space in your heart after holding on to it for what it seems a lifetime. One day you were convinced it was from God. You saw God in everything. And you felt God in everything.

It seemed to justify being with that person. Until one day God drops a clear no. One that can't fit your story. One that can't merge with your narrative. One that does not align with your hopes and plans for the future.

But friend, I've learned it's okay if deep down you still had hope for that relationship. If deep down you still wanted another chance. Deep down you had not grieved enough. Deep down you were still believing. Still wanting. Still hoping. Still making narratives. It shows your humanity. The readiness of your heart to love well. The openness to let someone in and love you back.

I want you to know that God does not hold it against you. He knew the outcome before you saw it coming. He knew how to protect you before you knew you needed protection. So grieve. Feel all the hurt. The pain. Let the space that person occupied in your heart grow smaller and smaller. And once it shrinks, then let go. But don't let go as a sign of defeat. Let go with your hands open to receive the true gift that lies ahead.

92

I Hope You Allow Yourself To Feel

If you have trouble processing feelings alone, this is for you.

Friend,

I hope you allow yourself to feel. Feel those times you were rejected. Those times you were misunderstood. Those times when you felt you did not fit in. And those times you were overlooked. You see, God is near and ready to heal. Once you invite Him in, there is no heart He will leave hurting. No heart He will leave broken. No heart He will leave empty. That's who He is. Jehovah Rapha, the One who heals.

I'm not saying it was not painful and unfair, but in the midst of all, He was close. He saw you. He never forsook you. He was protecting you. He had you. It might not make sense how He was in it. It might not make sense how He protected you. But remember, our God can use anything for our good. He uses our weaknesses to prove Himself strong. He uses the foolish things of the world to shame the wise. So call upon Him. Let Him come in.

I hope you allow yourself to feel and let Him heal.

93

Hopeless

If you have ever fought to feel hopeful, this is for you.

Friend,

Be thankful for the times you had hope — even if it left quickly, I know it was hard work. I know it was costly. Be proud of the times you chose the feeling of expectation — instead of disappointment. I know it took all the strength you had left. I know it was a process of letting go of negative mindsets.

Know that you did the best you can. In the midst of the feelings you had, you chose hope. And that is an action to be honored. Know that God is proud of you. Every time you decided to fill yourself with the hope of glory instead of the impossibility of your situation. Know that God sees you. Every time you chose to cry those tears, just to go to the pain with Him. He saw it. He recorded it. He is well pleased with it.

In the middle of hopelessness, you can be hopeful because He is with you; He gives you the strength where you feel like you have none. He gives you joyful expectation when you feel like you only have disappointment.

I'm proud of you for trusting, believing, and finding hope.

94

Let Yourself Fall Apart

This is for the girl going through a season of transition.

Friend,

You might be spending time with God as you usually do, but you still feel like you need more. You still feel empty.

You might be praying and declaring, and you still feel antsy, unsettled.

You go about your day — same routine, same footsteps — and still feel like you are not doing enough.

You start doubting your calling. Your voice. Your impact.

Friend, I've been there and want to encourage you to press in.
Let it be uncomfortable.
Let it be unfiltered.
Let it be messy.
Let yourself fall apart.

Every piece is meaningful. Every piece is cherished. But every piece needs restoration. Strength. And rebuilding.

Let yourself fall apart because in the end, you know the One who is right there with you. Picking up the pieces and gluing you back together — stronger, empowered, and filled with His zeal.

95

Let Faith Rise Up

If things are not going as planned, this is for you.

> *"Let faith support us where reason fails, and we shall think because we believe, not in order that we may believe."*
> *-Tozer*

Friend,

I pray that when life doesn't go as planned or how God said it would go, you don't lose heart. I hope you don't let your heart harden — or build up walls. I hope you don't blame God or build resentment in your heart towards your Creator. Instead, learn to change your perspective and let hope rise up in your heart.

I hope those times make you have greater faith.
I hope those times make you wonder what God is up to.
I hope those times make you dream of how He is already working to make it better — even when it already feels worse.

But ultimately, I hope they make you feel secure — knowing that you can't figure out your God. Knowing that His ways are so much higher than yours that sometimes the process won't make sense; it won't add up.

Friend, I hope you make time to encourage your soul. Speak to it what God has said. Speak His nature into existence. Declare His goodness and faithfulness. And let hope rise up again.

Remember, we should not take trusting God for granted. It's a privilege how we get to have a faith and have a relationship with Him along the journey. It's a breath of fresh air. It gives life. And it builds up your strength.

96

Let Go of the Ashes

This is for the girl having a hard time letting go of a relationship that ended.

Friend,

I've been there.
Countless crying nights.
Feeling like you don't have any more tears left.
Blaming yourself for why it ended or simply not understanding why.

I've been there.
Replaying memories over and over.
Feeling like nothing can extinguish the pain.
Thinking of the could've, would've, and should-haves.

But what if pain comes with purpose? What if what the enemy means for evil God can use for our good? What if your deepest pain was meant to catapult you into your God-given purpose?

I encourage you, go through those emotions with Jesus. Invite Him to the pain. And once you have allowed yourself to grieve the relationship, speak to your feelings and make them align with the word of God.

You see, God can and has promised to give you beauty for those ashes, but you first have to let go of the ashes. Let go of that resentment. Let go of that pain. Let go of that dream with that person.

One thing I know, and that is that if God took something away, it's because He has something better. Do not lose heart. He's got your past, present, and future.

97

Let Him Satisfy You

This is for the girl whose been disappointed in putting her hope in things of this world.

Friend,

I hope you get to enjoy the God-given gifts of this world. I hope you get to enjoy the company of good friends — laugh at their silliness, enjoy their company, and make memories. I hope you get to find that person who cherishes you for who you are and experience love.

But even more, I hope you realize how, even though these gifts are good, there is a bigger gift — a more satisfying gift. A gift that has proved what true love is. A gift that has given his life for you — just to be close and have a relationship with you. And that gift is being fully exposed and known, yet still lavishly loved by this man called Jesus.

You see, he is the only person who can truly satisfy the longings, desires, and expectations of your heart. This man Jesus, who freely offers an endless spring of satisfying water that no man can offer. This man Jesus who offers unconditional love in the midst of your mistakes, setbacks, and disappointments. This man Jesus who was pierced, beaten and crucified to have direct access to your mind, emotions, and spirit. This man Jesus, who is living water and provides you daily bread.

Without him, you are incomplete. Without Him, you are insatiated. But with Him, you will thirst no more. You will be as full as with the richest of meals. Let Him in. Let Him be Lord of your life. You won't be disappointed.

98

Hidden But Not Forgotten

This is for the girl feeling unnoticed and hidden.

Friend,

I know you might feel forgotten. I know you might feel like you are unseen, unwanted, and unappreciated. I know you thought God had better plans for your life. I know what He has promised seemed better than reality. And I know you are tired of hoping, believing, and trusting.

But friend, may I dare suggest that maybe you are hidden? Maybe God cherishes your heart so much that He is being jealous for it — not wanting to share you with anyone else? Maybe God delights so much in you that He wants to keep you for himself a little bit longer.

You see, God has an appointed time for everything. Just like David, sometimes you have to be hidden before you are exposed to the world. Sometimes you have to be excluded from everyone else, uninvited to events and left out to be ready for God's call for your life.

I encourage you, get lost in God during your hidden season. Cherish your moments together. Don't resent the lack of praise of men, rather, delight in the fact that God's eyes are directly on you. Instead of thinking you are forgotten and unimportant, might it be that you are hidden?

99

You Are Extravagant

This is for the girl feeling less than and unworthy or simply needs a reminder of her worth.

Extravagant (adj): extremely or unreasonably high in price.[2]

Friend,

I know you might have had hurts, rejections, and disappointments. I know you might have had failed relationships or simply unmet expectations. Needless to say, I know these might have made you question your worth and value: "Am I pretty enough? Am I not worth the fight? Am I not interesting enough?"

But friend, those rejections, failures, and disappointments do not get to dictate your worth and value, and they certainly do not get to dictate your future. You see, Jesus — the Son of God — died for you just to have a relationship with you. He considered having you close worthy of dying on a cross. You are that worthy. You are that significant. Indeed, you are *extravagant*.

---

[2] https://www.merriam-webster.com/dictionary/extravagant

So when you start feeling worthless and want to settle for something less, remember: You were created by the most high God. A God that concerns himself with your every move to the point of having endless thoughts about you! He knows when you sit and when you rise. He knows when you lay down. He discerns your thoughts and discerns your words before you speak them out.

Friend, remember, your worth and value comes from what God says about you. And He says you are beautifully and wonderfully made. He says you are His daughter. And He says that you are a royal priesthood. Never forget it.

100

You Matter

This is for the girl feeling like she does not matter.

Friend,

I want to remind you today that you matter. Your presence matters. Your actions matter. Your thoughts about a situation matter. What you choose to do with your time matters.

You see, God has placed a unique purpose and desire in your heart with which you get to change the world with. There is no other person who can bring that type of Heaven to Earth.

And yes, I know you might have let the world define you, give you identity, and a purpose. I know sometimes you might feel worthless and as if you have to try too hard to fit in.

But friend, let me remind you how you are not of this world. You were created to transform it and bring people to Jesus, but not to be accepted and get validation from it.

You see, the more you go to Jesus, the more He will speak identity, worth, and value over you. And as you go to Him, He will reveal great and unsearchable things you know nothing of. He will reveal the good works He has prepared for you to walk into.

So when you feel small. When you feel like you have no purpose. When you feel insignificant. Go to Him and let Him show you His blueprint for your life.

www.ingramcontent.com/pod-product-compliance
Lightning Source LLC
Chambersburg PA
CBHW062101080426
42734CB00012B/2712